DOWN YOUR WAY

Towns and villages around Salisbury

DOWN YOUR WAY

Towns and villages around Salisbury

by Alison Kidd

Foreword by Pamela Street

Drawings and design
by Graham Bleathman

Recent photographs by
Henry Wills
David Smith
Roger Elliott

Based on the Salisbury Journal Series

Volume One

First published in 1988 by

The Salisbury Journal,
8-12 Rollestone Street,
Salisbury,
Wiltshire,
SP1 1DY.

Second edition 1989

Edited by Gareth Weekes.
Typeset by David James and Sue Warne.

Printed by The Bath Press, Bath.

ISBN 0 9513920 0 X

Dedication: To everyone who helped, from the rich man in his castle to the poor man at his gate . . .

Contents

ERRATUM: In the chapter on Shrewton, the following line is missing from the top of the text on page 89: "Near the enormous grain drier dominating the skyline . . ."

Foreword

by Pamela Street

IT IS never easy to bring a place or a person to life on the written page in a strictly limited number of words. But in her study of villages in the Salisbury area, Alison Kidd has achieved this with remarkable skill. Down Your Way is based on articles in the Salisbury Journal which have appeared over a period of 18 months. It is neither a guide book nor an architectural appreciation. It is a portrayal of past and present communities, in which the human element comes over with great charm, enhanced by personal conversations and excellent photographs.

One common denominator which seems to link the series together is the unmistakable pride which the inhabitants of each village have in their particular little piece of England. "Whether you've lived here for one year or a hundred," the rector of Winterslow is quoted as saying, "it's your village if you are living here now."

I have never been able to understand why pride is considered one of the seven deadly sins. I am tremendously proud to have been born and brought up during the 1920s and 30s in what was then the little town of Wilton, near Salisbury. Alison Kidd's articles make it abundantly clear that, despite the inevitable changes which have taken place, especially within the living memory of those people with whom she spoke, this pride is as active today as it was nearly a century ago.

The community spirit is still thriving, admirably borne out by all the countless clubs and group activities, such as raising money for the church, campaigning against property developers, upholding ancient traditions, visiting the sick and elderly, attending lively Women's Institute or Parish meetings and supporting the local historian — for every village seems to have one — in his or her research.

In 1939, my late father, A. G. Street, after riding along the high ridge of downs between the Ebble and Nadder valleys, wrote:

I looked down on the cosy villages below. I thought of their past history and the many changes which it had brought to them . . . In every big change mankind both gains and loses . . . We cannot stop this change . . . We must watch it happen, but in so doing we should also watch carefully that in the process we do not lose something more precious than the thing we gain, something which, when once destroyed, we can never replace — that sleepy, lovely English village, even today the real heart of England.

Fifty years later, Alison Kidd's book helps to remind us of that charge and the watch which so many southern moonrakers are keeping to preserve the English village — now often threatened and certainly not quite as sleepy — yet still the real heart of England, dating from time immemorial.

Pamela Street.

The Villages

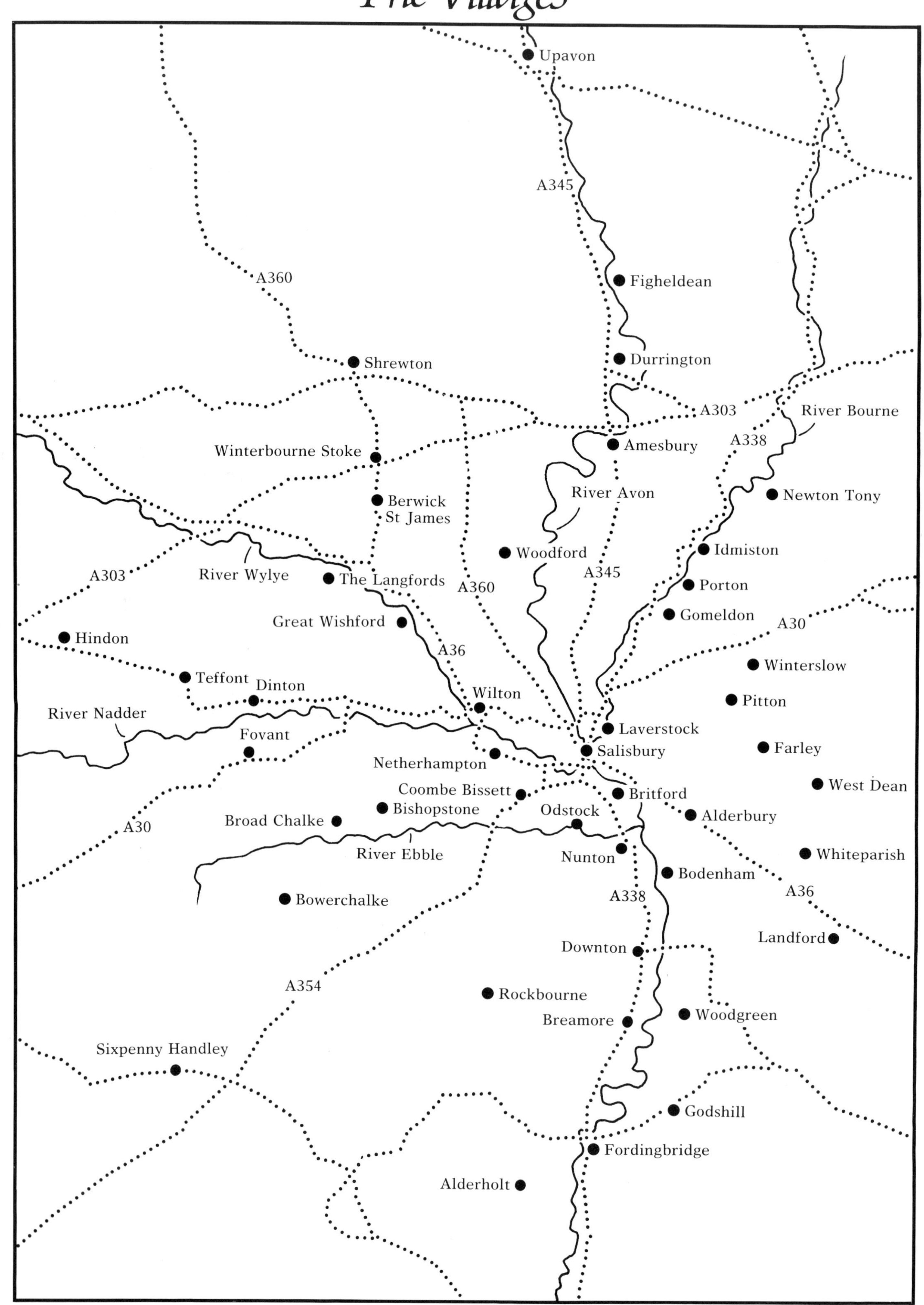

Introduction

"Just try to capture the flavour of a village." (My editor).

"You must be crazy." (My friends).

I CAME to the timelessness of Salisbury's villages with the naive curiosity of a child of Africa. The articles for the Salisbury Journal were just brief glimpses, like a holiday snapshot. A vivid first impression. Not a historical work.

I was asked to do each village "in a day" between October 1986 and April 1988. In each I found a guardian angel to pilot me, cups of coffee to revive me and yellowing photographs to copy.

But of course, I left people out. I was misinformed. Storms raged by the parish pump.

Fragile and unreal like sunlight on a dragonfly seem those tales of a stable world where you stayed in your village and knew your place, where you curtseyed in the street and went into service and, when times got bad, "you managed".

Not only has the old village lifestyle gone. The old villagers are dying. Many died in the weeks before their "Down Your Way" story appeared. And they were the ones who told me how to cut a pig's throat and salt it, how to black a range and cook on it, and how you mixed nightsoil with ashes by the light of the moon.

It was seldom in a thatched cottage that I found those robust country faces. So often they and their children have had to move away. Tales of winter farmyard evenings and the family tin bath sound far-fetched in push-button council bungalows. But they are precious. They are more than dewy-eyed nostalgia.

So if I have touched lightly on the stately home and the weekenders, the bridge club, playgroup and the plaster gnomes, it's because 700 weekly words have made me selective. The new village life is authentic, too, but I suspect we'll have it for longer.

In those living memories I found a unique flavour in each of these villages. Thank you to everyone who helped me do it. Just in time. It has been fun.

Alison Kidd,
September 1988.

Alderbury

"Alderbury without a Prewett is like a pudding without suet" went the old saying, and today there is not a single Prewett left in Alderbury or Whaddon.

There are Newmans and Riches, Ernies and Occomores; Earls of Radnor at Longford Castle and Christie-Millers at Clarendon House but most of the names, like the houses, are new.

At night the big new developments — the 260 dwellings built by Wimpey and the 64 higher up the hill — are marked out with street lights.

The rest of the village, apart from the pubs, police and telephone kiosk, is happily wrapped in darkness.

It is tempting at night to picture the ghosts of Augustinian 12th century Priors at Ivychurch, the Plantagenet kings deep in Clarendon forest and the 64 Saxon skeletons at Petersfinger — a corruption of "Peter ad vincula".

Alderbury and Whaddon have grown suddenly (and merged). There were 741 people in 1841 and slightly fewer 100 years later. By 1971 they had grown to 1,117 and today there are about 1,800 on the electoral roll.

Surface water flooding in winter shows the strain and there are strongly-expressed views on further development.

Today's children attend the same Victorian school (plus overflow huts) as those rural youngsters of long ago. But there's a new school in the pipeline for the 1990s.

Colourful scenes from Alderbury's past come easily to Parish Council chairman, Bob Newman, whose roots go back four generations in Alderbury.

"I remember open day at the school. There were the parents dressed in their best with the men from Hampshire Cleansing carrying their full buckets from the toilets past them . . ."

"Do you remember how our well-loved parson, Chris Pooley, used to frighten the over-60s to death when he gave them lifts in his old Bedford Dormobile . . .?"

At the Guy Fawkes bonfire, built with Clarendon wood, "when my son was only a nipper, John Eynon picked up a piece of wood like a pit prop and threw it. It went clean over the pile and hit my son on the head."

The Dowager Countess of Radnor and Mrs Winifred Garrett at work on the famous Pleydell-Bouverie carpet.

Pugin's romantic St Marie's Grange, built in 1835 when he was 23.

Alderbury's emblem — the fountain on the village green.

Methodists and Anglicans unite: Methodist steward Ethel Occomore, Rev. Gordon Mitchell and Deaconess Christina Hunt in front of St Mary's in 1986.

Below: Bob Newman (right) chairman of Alderbury Parish Council, with his father, Norman, at Oakwood Grove, the village's newest housing estate.

Fred Witt ended up in hospital with no hair on his arms after "using some kind of spirit to start the fire."

Despite the influx of newcomers (or because of them?) Alderbury has an astonishing community life. Here the Salvation Army first had a brass band. There's a fine record of co-operation between Methodists and Anglicans, Roman Catholics and Baptists. The Sunday Schools overflow.

From cradle to grave, "it's all go" — Mothers and Toddlers, Playgroups, Cubs, Brownies, 75 years of Guiding (28 Queens Guides), Scouts, Youth Club, Mothers Union, Wives Group, WI, Gardening Club and the Friendly Club for the Over-60s.

For the sporty, there is tennis, badminton, cricket and "county-standard" bowls. Others prefer the choir, or the Alderbury Singers.

And three tireless local needlewomen have chosen a unique labour of love. Thursday afternoons for them are devoted to helping embroider the famous 18ft by 12½ft Pontremolli-designed carpet for the Dowager Countess of Radnor at Avonturn in Lower Alderbury.

"It's like a Chinese wallpaper design," says Winifred Garrett. "We work every stitch twice because the needle has three threads and we want the effect of six. Only the petit point has two strands. It gives a 3-D effect." Thousands of visitors came to see the carpet last summer.

Though there's no local doctor, there's a village bobby, a fine council estate "Spider's Island", two shops and a pub at each end of the village.

The Green Dragon is claimed by Dickens fans for Martin Chuzzlewit's "Blue Dragon". Certainly, Dickens used to visit Alderbury, crossing from Britford by ½d ferry. ("Miss Hazel's father used to work that ferry.")

The Three Crowns today looks anything but regal with a red London bus outside, playhouses on stilts and climbing frames. But some time has elapsed since King Edward III went out hunting with his "Prisoners" — Kings David of Scotland and John of France, who gave the pub the name.

And on the Village Green — a blend of old and new like all of this tolerant village — today stands an animal drinking fountain dated 1902 built from pieces of Ivychurch cloister by a village grateful to the Radnors for a water supply. It has become the village emblem.

Alderholt

ALDER trees, wild heathland and a mill — that's all that's known of Alderholt until 1330.

Then the potteries began. Small farmers in this remote outpost of the Earls of Salisbury's estates began making wheel-turned, lead-glazed rural earthenware from the clay, sand and wood on the common (marked "Bruere Commune" on the old maps).

They were mostly Majors and Hennings, those old potting families. John Major, the younger, is immortalised for fathering the baby born to Mary Welch, widow, in 1702. He was found dead in an earthen pot (measuring 14in x 8ins) in a pottery shed. But most Alderholt utensils were used for cooking and eating.

Tony Light, archeologist, says the Alderholt industry was at its peak between 1650 and 1750. In 1880 the railway and mass-produced ware from the Midlands killed the last two kilns. Verwood potteries lasted a little longer.

The huge mound on Peter Gould's Salisbury Arms Farm contains kiln upon kiln, insulated with earth and ancient pottery shards. He found a 15-inch diameter pipe still full of (dry) 17th century soot. Slim bricks from a 17th century drying shed lie nearby.

There were practical reasons for putting early kilns here near Pressey's corner and today's Moonacre restaurant. This was the edge of the wild heathland. Kilns needed clay, sand and wood and had a built-in fire risk. The potters' homes were built some way off, the earliest around "the green."

Later came brickmaking. In 1580 Robert Childe was at work. Visit the DIY Surplus Stores to see old brick ovens. Older ones, found while digging foundations on the other side of the railway, have (like most of the pottery kilns) recently been destroyed. Barry Wallis, undertaker, keeps Alderholt's photo record.

The old Station Hotel became the Churchill Arms. Its name came from Squire George Onslow Churchill at Alderholt Park (50 acres) who granted permission for the railway line to be built across his land. In exchange Alderholt got its own Daggons Road station.

Barry Wallis' great grandfather was there watching on Thursday, December 20, 1866, when the first train arrived. Ninety-eight years later, on May 2, 1964, Stan Broomfield could be seen climbing aboard the last (6pm) Weymouth West Country Class train with a tape recorder built into his suitcase.

They used to say "Angels walked up the front" of the 1849 church of St James (150 sittings). Today they are treating it for dry rot. Like the green corrugated Reading Room, the church was a gift of the Marquis of Salisbury, the Lord of the Manor based at Cranborne.

He'd lend his car and chauffeur for a hospital visit. He also used to visit his tenants. For some a pint and a pipe was enough. But he'd discuss world affairs with Charlie Ford, who read a newspaper every night by oil lamp.

In those feudal days, Alderholt had more shops ("remember Pressey's bread and Percy Palmer?") and you knew everyone. "Going to town" meant a trip to Fordingbridge and you went to dances by horse and cart.

In 1847 they built a "mudwalled school" enlarged in 1874 to take 156 pupils. It became a Youth Club when the new £1½-million first school was built. Today it has six teachers and 170 children who move on to higher schools at Cranborne and then Wimborne.

In Edith Pinhorn's time, when schoolboys wore knee-length breeches and long socks, bearded school-

Above: The late Len Lane and his son Peter, local hurdlemakers, demonstrated their craft at local agricultural shows.

Left: Barry Wallis, aviation enthusiast and local historian, with his favourite view of Alderholt, copied from an old postcard.

Below: Peter Gould of Salisbury Arms Farm, the last dairy farmer in the village, shows the difference in thickness between modern and 17th century bricks at the ancient pot kiln in his farmyard.

Above: Daggons Road Station in 1907.

master George Mann (who doubled as Parish Clerk) would often slip an urchin half a crown for new hose. Today there's no sign of poverty.

In 1903 Alderholt and its hamlets had only a dozen private homes. There were farmers, sheep trough makers and higglers, brick and drain makers, hedgers, hurdlemakers, coalmen and craftsmen. Postmaster Tom Brewer was woodman to Squire Churchill and Mr Oliver ran the station.

Now Peter Lane is the only one making hurdles, since the recent death of his father, Len. "We'll keep it going till the wood runs out." The Earlswood walking stick maker has downed tools and, Barry Wallis says, the glow-worms have gone from Station Road.

There are still a few small farmers battling with the weather and the EEC milk quotas. But mostly it's new build and new faces. There are still muddy lanes but Alderholt today has an urban flavour.

The population changed little (689 in 1901) until the 1972 development plan. "With the arrival of the sewer, Alderholt took off." Today like a small town, its population is over 3000 and still growing. Houses are sold before they are built. Some change hands twice a year.

Stan White, still newsagent after 26 years, put it succinctly: "It used to be nice and quiet and friendly. Now it's just friendly."

Left: Coronation celebrations at Alderholt in 1911.

Right: Pupils and teachers at the old Alderholt School in Cranborne Road in 1910.

OVER 66 years, Amanda Harris has seen Alderholt transformed. A wartime dispatch rider rode right through Alderholt without noticing. No-one could miss it today.

"They're like sardines in a tin," one farmer said to me.

"In the old days, we were known for Pottery and Poverty," Amanda says, "but people were proud. They managed."

They all had a pig and a couple of cows and would cut hedges for the faggots. A badger skin fetched a shilling.

At Cripplestyle and Crendell, old ladies knitted yellow hunting gloves by oil lamp. Mr Harding, the butcher, delivered in all weathers ("He kept the meat in a little box under the seat") and Herbie Nicklen brought groceries from Damerham on a bicycle.

The fire under the copper heated water for your weekly bath as well as the laundry. You "began with the whites" but one tubful did the lot. ("Blue them, boil them, mangle and starch them." No wonder washing took all day Monday.)

On Saturday, Ted Saunders' springless bus went to Salisbury and you hung on outside if it was full. His Mystery Tours were "wild treats". So were the crisps and fizzy lemonade.

Alex Butler, Amanda's farmer father, was an unforgettable character. He'd leave the cows half milked and join the hunt as he was, if he heard the hounds in full cry.

"He once brought a donkey upstairs," Amanda says. "The donkey kept trying to kick his reflection in the mirror. They crashed downstairs together."

Miss Hardwick, the tennis player, lived at The Pines, the Miss Bullers on the Ringwood Road, General Gordon was on the outskirts and "we had Lady Smith-Gordon." If you visited Mrs McIntosh, of course you used the kitchen door.

Then the war arrived. Suddenly Alderholt was full of soldiers. For the village girls, "it was Christmas every day."

Alderholt (once Padner) Mill on the Hampshire-Dorset boundary has seen some changes, too. Ann and John Pye restored it six years ago. There you can admire the old machinery, the cogs and the stones, the chatterbox and damsel, the undershot 1840 wheel outside with its great paddles. "Only the horse is not original," Ann says.

The Mill's craft shop is overflowing with local talent — from the home-ground flour and Christopher Pye's fudge, to scarves and jewellery. There's glass engraving, too, and three-weekly art exhibitions. "We're already booked up for next year."

"We may not be a pretty village, but there's something about Alderholt," they said to me.

Teenagers felt differently. "There's not a lot for us to do. You need a car to get out. There aren't even any clothes shops." Maybe so. But at least they don't have to cycle to nightschool in Ringwood, like Amanda Harris did, pushing her bike through the flooded meadows at Ibsley Bridge.

Above: The scene nearly 80 years ago as pupils make their way to the old school in Cranborne Road.

Above right: Girl meets boy in 1910.

Right: The quaint village church of St James, one of four in the parish. "Angels used to climb up those steps," children were told.

Left: Ron and Barbara Hood with their well-loved steam road roller which they exhibit at the Alderholt Steam-Up and other rallies.

Below: The 1956 Alderholt Pantomime, Jack and The Beanstalk, one of the series for which the village has made a name for itself.

Amanda Harris, well-known in the village for her role as grand dame in the annual pantomimes, outside her old school, now the youth club.

Every night of the week there is frenetic activity in the Youth Centre, Village Hall or Reading Room. There's the skittle alley at the Hall and Woodhouse pub, there's the children of Alderholt Drama Group, two WIs and a wives group, voluntary cars, badminton and dog training, art and dancing, pantomimes and music, a Friendship club, chiropody, clinics, Beavers, Scouts, Brownies and Guides ... There's also the Moonacre Restaurant.

The Rev Stephen Abram is Vicar, the Rev Dennis Scurrell is Congregational Minister. Both live in Alderholt and there's a joint annual carol service in the Village Hall with the Methodists and the Full Gospel church.

Outsiders come to Alderholt to buy pet food or to visit the amazing emporium — Alderholt Surplus Stores. An elderly fire engine on the forecourt reminds one of the huge November 1986 blaze. Once inside the fireproof warehouse (reopened May 1987), you can find everything from a zip to a door, carpets, baths, bikes, windows and Christmas crackers.

Others seek out the nurseries, the mechanics, or Valerie Sillence's made-to-measure exclusive Hillbury knitwear. ("It's a hobby gone mad.")

Twelve thousand visitors attend Ron Hood's annual Alderholt Steam Rally on the first weekend in August. Though it's not held in the village, "it's the one thing that really draws us all together," Stan Broomfield says. "All the money is for charity and it all goes back into Alderholt."

The shops are scattered here and there. But Alderholt has a grocer, post office, butcher, hair-dresser, newsagent and even a TV showroom. It has its own undertaker and a vet. The flag flies at the War Memorial every Sunday. There are 14-acres of sports fields and a rifle range.

It's a little odd to be in Dorset, have your mail sorted in Hampshire and use a Wiltshire postcode. But 3,000 people like the way Alderholt is moving. And it's still growing.

Berwick St James

BERWICK HOUSE was decorated with ivy and holly. At 2.30 am on Christmas Eve the village carol singers with storm lanterns formed a huge circle on the lawn, "Awake, Awake, Awake, Awake . . ." they sang.

The children of the big house, woken and wrapped in eiderdowns, watched enthralled until silence fell and the singers crept away. The next night at 6 there was wassail in the drive.

Berwick St James no longer welcomes Christmas this way. But to this day the unrecorded indigenous carols composed by Jonah Blanchard are sung secretly by his descendants in nearby Shrewton. No-one else knows the words.

There were other Berwick traditions — Gardener Harry Emm always made a Yuletide ashen faggot. ("Did you know ash can burn wet or dry.") As each bond snapped off there was a toast, starting with the Royal Family. There were village cocktails on Twelfth Night and unforgettable concerts in Parsonage Farm.

"My father sang 'A Yard of Lace', and 'I can't keep my beastly eyeglass in'," says Diana Gifford Mead. Rene Gant would play the piano, Harold Draper sang and there were WI sketches on winter evenings.

School leavers began work by bird-scaring. You ate your onion-and-cheese dinner with a penknife under a hayrick and at harvest time there was cider at 6.

Today's Berwick still has two major farms (Bucknells at Manor Farm, Streets at Berwick Hill) and 187 people. In 1801 it had 226. It has one main street ("not surfaced since they brought in mains water"), 27 at the school and, being without street lights, no speed limit.

The walls of the unpretentious dampish Norman church "weep for the blighted hopes of the young" says the guide book and the porch gates are specially designed to exclude pigs.

Twelve acres of conservation meadow attract summer study groups. They all like to shop at the Post Office run by the Odds — latest successors to bewhiskered Tom Kitley (shopkeeper 1871-1939) whose cob house fell into the street one memorable day in the 1950s.

Wadsworth's beer addicts and pony-trekkers patronise the Boot, where once you could have your shoes mended while you supped.

Mrs Hilda Bucknell, of Manor Farm, explains to grandson Humphrey, how shoes were made in the farm smithy in the days before tractors.

The interior of the church with its original font.

Above: The famous Serpentine Wall at Berwick House (seen here in the 1930s) is one of three left in England.

Right: Old Tom Kitley who ran the village shop from 1880 to 1930, seen in retirement.

Below: Mrs Diana Gifford Mead in the water meadows by the mill.

The local corn mill was even more versatile than the pub. It was a beanmill from early times and new machinery came from Shrewton in 1810. It diverted water to the drowned meadows ("they were safe for sheep if there was no 'r' in the month"). It pumped water for the locals, it made ("dim") electricity and, with a shaft and cogwheel, even did the churning.

Though no longer thatched, modern Berwick is still full of cob walls and largely tenanted. Its Lords have included Ashburton, Pembroke and Malmesbury, the Duchy of Lancaster and gentlemen farmers like Furness and Collins (Master of Wylye Hunt).

Flamboyant speculator E. T. Hooley, who owned the Royal Yacht Britannia, also bought the village. He left his pavement incomplete when he went bankrupt in 1898.

D-Day parachute rehearsals caught the villagers unprepared. "All we were told was that electricity would be cut off. Then came that parachute "invasion." I hid the pram under a hayrick as motorbikes and jeeps suddenly came tumbling down!" Mrs Gifford Mead remembers.

"The lie of the land is like Arnhem," says Will Hibberd, blacksmith's son.

Today's villagers, headed by Hilda Bucknell, visit the housebound and elderly. Parish issues like the bungalow-turned-house and the bypass are discussed in the thatched reading room ("A parish meeting, not a council").

Near Muddy Lane stand two Sarsen stones, stolen from Stonehenge to keep long-ago feet dry, but Berwick's 13th century chalice is in the British Museum.

Salisbury Museum has their 17lb Great Bustard, shot January 25, 1871, the last of its kind. With an 80-inch wingspan, "it made good eating".

The Blanchards, Dyers, Mundys, Williams and Rolfes have left. (It was Bill Williams who trapped a polecat in 1937). "From 1939 it has been an entirely new village," says Rev John Adams. Tiny it may be but there's a playgroup, darts team and fete.

It's a newcomer, Nicky Street, who is currently lifting the dust and disturbing the ghosts. And ghosts there are. Mrs Dibden saw a swishing-skirted lady in the Old School House after laying out Mr Ward. There's also a midnight walker from Uppington pub.

Nicky is writing-up the village, beginning with Yarnbury castle 300 BC, Roman brooches and coins and the prehistoric British "with very bad teeth and chronic arthritis".

"Berwick" means "outlying barley farm" and added "St James" in 1190 to please Queen Matilda, King Stephen's rival. James of Compostella was her favourite saint — she even gave Reading Abbey his hand as a relic.

Bishopstone

THIS IS A village with a woodland wilderness, where a maid once loved a snake and pined and died when her father killed it . . . a village of 495 people with a bus but no school, spreading desultorily along the Ebble valley, its fertile watermeadows rising to high chalk downs.

Bishop Wordsworth's widow lived here, so did Rev Augustus Montgomery, prototype for Trollope's Dr Grantly. A donkey once pulled the rector's lawnmower, someone kept 256lb of cheese in his lounge and Rev Montgomery, always particular about building standards, was killed by a falling wall.

It's been a compassionate village (even in 1500 there were 4d bequests to the poor) and by 1833 Widow Baker was allowed a furze faggot and Robert Baker a shirt but no stockings.

Rev Bromley, one of Bishopstone's rare vicars-in-residence, was a saintly man. He built a house for the poor, and somehow survived himself in a damp rectory despite "delicate health, rheumatic complaints and liableness to spasms". Despite his efforts, 1838 agricultural conditions drove 68 of 560 villagers to Australia.

Today Bishopstone stretches from the Blandford Road to the Race Plain. Six tiny hamlets date back to Saxon manors — Flamston, Netton and Bishopstone Manor on the north bank and Croucheston, Faulston and Throope on the south. But they work well together.

All the "big houses" are interesting. Fortified stone-walled Faulston House was the grandest manor, had a deer park and became a Roundhead headquarters. "Its dovecot is all that remains of four 14th century defensive towers," says Elizabeth Gallop, prizewinning historian. "There's no sign of moat or wall".

Before the days of death duties, landowners clung tenaciously to Bishopstone — Winchester Cathedral held it from 676 to 1551 when Henry VIII began the Pembroke's rule. They stayed until 1947. But the Marquis of Abergavenny only lasted nine years and today it's the Duke of Newcastle's domain.

In the 60s he built 28 modern houses in the Croft. Despite misgivings over these "townies", their energies are to be found everywhere from Cue One's plays, to church working parties and Keep Fit. Ken Lorrain's inventive fundraising schemes for the church and village hall have paid the bills, too.

Both the District Council and the villagers have rejected Newcastle Estates' latest controversial plans to move all its farmland to the north of the main road — exchanging a Netton Farm field for the playing fields.

The school (founded 1837, closed 1974) remains a house. There Stan Barter bribed girls with sweets to win the 1900 Good Fellowship prize. There the 1899 assistant mistress "behaved improperly" with a farmer and wartime Portsmouth evacuees shocked the country children.

Methodists share upkeep, responsibilities and communion at St John the Baptist's church and recently paid for new heating. The organ Frank Gulliver played for 50 years has been done up.

It's a fine church reminiscent of Downton, with rooks cawing in the churchyard, a carved priest's door and a dear little unexplained cloister. There's a stained-glass saint with two left feet, civil war bullet holes in the West door and some fine woodwork and tombs.

Don't believe the guide book. The Black Death, Death, says Elizabeth Gollop, caused no sudden evacuation panic. The village spread slowly over 100 years.

Above: After 48 years in the trade, master thatcher Phil Dimmer at work. The old school is in the background.

Left: Churchwarden Ken Lorrain and the old Priest's door at the Church.

Below: Faulston House with its pre-Reformation flint and stone dovecot.

Farmer Ted Draper outside The Three Horseshoes, where he was born.

Bishopstone welcomes warm humid weather for it makes watercress grow. It's a Barter family business. His father, Stanley, switched to beekeeping each summer, but since the 60s Norman has grown watercress all the year round. His Bishopstone beds are England's seventh biggest.

Fed by a spring 250ft deep and carefully hand-picked, they supply markets from Leeds to Cardiff. Most "chips" are transported by night, ice-packed in cool lorries.

At Croucheston Mill they grind animal feeds, but access for lorries is over a slimline bridge. New red brick houses are packed in nearby. A 14-year-old's 1945 match-and-petrol-can experiment finished off the old water mill ("the house used to shake when the wheel turned") but there's centuries-old mill machinery in Captain Murray's Faulston home and stone hatches in the streams.

At Netton Farm they once sold beer through a hole in the wall and merrymakers ended up before the magistrates. Today it's available from the White Hart and Three Horse Shoes. The latter is worth finding.

It's unspoilt and full of old stories in Wiltshire accents. Ted Draper (who was born in the pub) remembers the Woodbine-filled voice of Charlie Dimmer asking, "Going to stand I one you? (= will you stand me one?) and old Sam Spicer constantly interrupting with, "Thee's know my meaning you?"

This is where Tom Salmon, the basketmaker, used to soak withies in the Ebble. Nearby row of thatched cottages was demolished. First an American tank knocked off their porches. Later, as Bill Lanham says, "the whole front fell out of 'Quiet Alice's' house. We saw it going to school."

That's no doubt why Frank Draper used to say, "If you dislike anyone, leave them a thatched cottage."

Today here, as elsewhere, they are sought-after—and thatcher Phil Dimmer (like his father) is constantly in demand.

Below: Bishopstone choir outing in the 1920s.

Bodenham

OF the three Radnor villages — Odstock, Nunton and Bodenham — Bodenham is the smallest, the closest to the fairytale castle and unashamedly feudal.

It has 56 people "including the children" in its single street and only one new house has been built there since the war.

Amputated from its sisters by the A338, it has neither school, church nor pub and lost its chapel in August. But it has a thriving shop and the Radnor Hall is sprucely painted.

On the balcony, the badges of Bodenham's wartime regiments bring back the days when Americans took over New Hall, Longford Park was full of tents and huts and Montgomery stayed at the castle.

The street runs down to the shining river. On one side is Longford. On the other stands the New Hall of 1881. (From 1700 New Halls kept burning down.) This is the one Ursula Olivier (born Buckley) lived in as a child. There were staff prayers, a library of bound dark red books and lots of ticking clocks.

"I remember one night leaning over the gallery and screaming and nobody hearing," she says. Tea in the servant's hall "was the greatest treat" and Mummers acted Dumb Crambo in the hall on Christmas Eve.

Since 1980, New Hall, once home to John Creasey and the Buckleys, has been a private hospital under Joyce Harvey, matron. (37 beds, two theatres, more than 12,000 patients). The original stables, reception rooms, proud trees and rolling lawns survive. From there you can see Lord Folkestone's (octagonal) Round House.

Before cars came to Bodenham you had time to gossip with Mr Male at his gate, every house had rambler roses in front, beautiful gardens behind — and earth closets at the bottom.

Violet Beale remembers 40 children spilling out of the chapel and the flower show in the park ("swing boats and threading needle races . . . laugh!").

Countrymen like Toddler Tucker will still find you mushrooms and primroses. Many villagers have worked all their lives "for his Lordship" and "won't hear a word against him".

Only since 1970 have outsiders moved in. Consultants, Queen's Messengers, butlers, gamekeepers . . . you meet them all in the Hobbs' cosy Post Office.

Peter Jenkins, Lord Radnor's agent for nearly 30 years, lends his fine garden every other year for "the

Below: New Hall, now a busy hospital catering for private patients.

Right: John Creasey, the crime writer, at work in his study at New Hall, where he wrote Toff and the Inspector West thrillers.

Below: Bodenham Mill.

The modernised Longford Castle firemen, with their motor pump.

Right: Peter Jenkins, Lord Radnor's agent for 30 years.

Below: Longford Castle illuminated for a concert during Salisbury Festival.

Fete of the three Peters". They raised £2,229 last June.

He'd rather talk of that than share any headaches involved in caring for the forest, the farms, woods, fish farms, houses, cottages, pubs, shops, sporting fishing, and shooting that come into the Earl's domain.

"In the exalted position of Keeper of the Gate" to Longford Castle is Bob Stone, Methodist lay preacher and castle butler for 16 years.

From "following the plough in Downton, look you," he found himself in St James' Palace as gentleman's gentleman. This valet had never seen a bath with taps before or a toilet with a chain. ("I thought it was a footbath," he says).

You need a permit to visit the 1592 castle grounds. Flag flying over the turrets, Longford Castle is straight out of a storybook. With circular towers and a moat, it was built in a triangle by Sir Thomas Gorges with Spanish treasure. Cromwell took it in 1695. In 1717, Sir Edward des Bouveries bought it from the Coleraines, and began adding to it. By 1876, it had become a hexagon.

The ancient "Long Ford" in the Avon is still visible, and so is the bridge that moved. The chequerboard estate office, built as a Royal hunting box for Clarendon Palace, is older than the castle, though dwarfed by it. The famous fire escape on wheels was recently used to repair its tower, but no-one is presently recruiting for another private fire brigade.

In the mill lives Molly Riddlestone, daughter of the old riverkeeper, Victor Hawtin, "who taught Lord Radnor to fish". He'd have died for the Radnors, she says.

Like today's Andy Grey, Victor captained the Saturday cricket matches in front of the castle and his wife, Mabel, scored and ran the Monday night dances at the Radnor Hall.

In those days the rivermen wore breeches, gaiters and waders and the agent, Mr Kyle, was remote and untouchable. Twice a year, the woodmen would cut the weeds with knives on ropes across the river. It was four men's work to keep the castle paths tidy.

Here time stands still. The 8th Earl comes riding past. Wildfowl abound and wild deer. They remember waving flags for Queen Mary (who ignored them) and the present Queen (who didn't).

For those within the pale of the park, there are still carols in the castle hall on Christmas Eve . . . unforgettable under an immense Christmas tree with real candles.

Everything about Longford is out of another world.

Bowerchalke

TUCKED protectively into the Ebble valley is pretty scattered Bowerchalke, named for the Atte Burgh family.

It boasts a stud and a thatcher, a trout farm and a vineyard, farmers Mann, Rawle and Beckley, hamlets with quaint names like Misselfore and Chase, 329 people, a busy village hall, pub, church, chapel and shop.

Here you may meet violinist Iona Brown, Sir Richard Pitman (ex-MP) or John Russell, head of Odstock's Spinal Unit. Here David Cecil gave his last performance and they filmed part of Barry Lyndham. Novelist William Golding and rocket scientist Jim Lovelock have left their mark. But its real celebrity is the generous, enterprising Edward Collett who became curate in 1878 (d.1924).

Research on him began with Rex Sawyer unearthing candelabra, photographic plates, tools and bottles under the Vicarage cedar tree. Soon it will make a book.

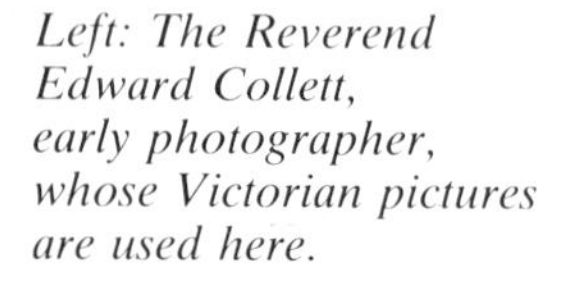

Left: The Reverend Edward Collett, early photographer, whose Victorian pictures are used here.

Below: Dr Hayden and family, 1885.

Sergeant Wallace in 1889.

For this was some country clergyman. Tender-hearted, sexist, he chid the Pembrokes over frogs in Quidham Street water, provoked a public (barn) meeting on Baptism, served soup, loved gipsies and was an early DIY photographer, journalist, printer and publisher. All on £100 a year.

The Parish Papers (Price 1/4d Eph. VI 22) measure 10" by 6" and cover affairs local, national and spiritual over 40 years. A full set is kept in the Bodleian. They have travelled the world.

Bowerchalke now gets one-sixth of a vicar. The Methodist Chapel is for sale. But the Baptists have a resident minister, Philip Savage, newly arrived.

Holy Trinity Church is worth a visit ... despite Wyatt's restoration. Sara Sawyer has catalogued the gravestones. Don't miss the steep climb to the cogwheels of the clock (W. Cannon, London 1880) wound with a heavy handle. Up there it smells greeny-damp.

At Pug's Hole on dark nights a ghostly shepherd cries from a thorntree. Mrs Thelma Barter saw the spectred grey-shawled Mrs Elliott at Woodminton. No birds sing near the Verditch grave of Kit, the gipsy suicide. There are tales of Verne Ditch, Sheppard's Cross and Applespill Bridge. Seven men drag a coffin and headless warhorses thunder by. The WI history tells all.

The main street runs up the valley. New infilling rubs fences with cob, brick and flint. The Merritts (not the long-serving Hapgoods) run the Bell Inn. At roof height David Laity can be seen knee-deep in golden thatch.

Too many foreigners for Fred Penny. His grandfather Charles set up the village shop as a squatter, father sold 6/11d heavy boots ("they'd last a year") and Fred ran the business for 40 years through the

Above: The Bell Inn at Bowerchalke.

Right: Bowerchalke carrier, 1884.

Above: Fred Penny, who ran the village shop for 40 years.

Left: Douglas Mann and Mark Thompson, partners in Chalkhill Wines, a flourishing new Bowerchalke industry.

days of coupons and shortages.

He remembers Mrs Downs, the shepherd's wife, delivering babies, Tipcat played with a tin and hazel sticks, a donkey falling into Foyle's sawpit and a school roll of 84. Schoolmaster Penfound preferred music to the 3Rs. He had pupils outdoors measuring land with a chain and grafting fruit trees.

Mrs Gretta Adams, the last Bowerchalke schoolmistress, remembers evacuees and gasmask inspection, wartime folk dancing and "a great community spirit." But falling rolls closed the 1844 school in 1976. The dressing-up clothes went to Ebbesbourne Wake, but she still has soldiers' letters, pantomime pictures ("the boy who made that Cinderella coach is a carpenter today") and the Victorian records.

"We did our work by the sound of the playground voices," Mrs Monica Lee says. She was blessed by Edward Collett and inherited his treasures. Her uncle, John Linnell, arrived with him and stayed on as manservant, organist and village indispensable. But he was no match for the gipsies who, Fred Penny says, "brought the same baby to be christened six times, knowing they would get 1/-".

Much has changed in Bowerchalke. Marleycombe is timeless and Knowle Farm immaculate. There's riding and swimming — not Friendly Society feastdays or quoits. Old names stick — Hardiman, Foyle and Day (1703) Gulliver, Sheppard and Targett (1813). Poor Patch is still a charity though no one collects armfuls of fuel.

Read Bowerchalke Broadsheet for the Flower Show, Playgroup, and Day Centre. But it's not a patch on Rev Collet's. And it doesn't cost a farthing, either.

Above: William Golding, winner of the Nobel Prize for Literature, lived in Bowerchalke.

Right: Village indispensable, John Linnell, with his penny farthing in 1888.

Below: Bowerchalke in the snowy winter of 1889.

Breamore

Below: Born and bred in Breamore, Hubert Henstridge is Hayward of the Marsh.

THERE are many experts on Breamore, that remarkable tiny village on the west bank of the Avon with a 1,000-year-old church almost intact, a miz-maze, stocks, a Countryside Museum, the remains of a priory and a common called "the Marsh", all overlooked by an Elizabethan mansion.

As a delightful introduction to the village, I recommend the schoolchildren's blue exercise books for their mixture of fact and flavour.

The name "means the moor or marsh covered with broom ... Breamore Station today is a square overgrown smelly old place ... The tracks were ... made into razor blades. The bridge's underside is black where all the smoke has burnt it ..."

"When you're in Breamore Churchyard alone, it feels sacred because of the Yew trees ..."

"Today Breamore Priory is just a large field of long grass beside the River Avon, The old track is a grassish mud which squelches under your foot."

All the village helped the 68 pupils with their research. PC Otter came; Mr Mussell, line superintendent, talked about the long-ago railway with its mail train at ten-to-four and its first station master Robert Clasey. Mr Ponting spoke of his childhood.

Under headteacher, Keith Ford, they studied population statistics, the Hulse family tree, the school logbook (1927 — scarlet fever — Sidney and Winnie Slade excluded for 3 months) mazes, the church, monks and even the buses.

Those of more scholarly bent seek out market gardener, archaeologist and historian, Anthony Light, who has researched Breamore and reads medieval clerical scripts for fun.

He delights in Phillip Theryll's uncorrected handwritten 1515 will in Breamore dialect. He bequeaths "misol to bi berid afore howyraldi" (= our lady).

"It's just an ordinary rural community," he says. He'll direct you from its Neolithic long barrow to its Roman remains, medieval miz-maze and 96½ft Minster church AD 980 ("the most important Anglo-Saxon building in Hampshire" ... do you see two Runic letters in the writing of HER SWUTELATH SEO GECWYDRAEDNES THE?")

From the churchyard you get a splendid view of Breamore House, built in a great E in 1580 by unhappy William Dodington who was in 1600 to throw himself from the tower of St Sepulchre's church, Holborne. In 1629 a Dodington son murdered his mother. Another Dodington went blind.

Assuming these misfortunes stemmed from family guilt for buying priory lands, Dodingtons poured gifts on the church, built almshouses, and in 1639 set up a parson's trust deed. The Breamore House family — since 1748 the Hulses — still appoint him.

Summer tourists (28,000 last year) throng to admire the magnificently-furnished rooms hung with great portraits. "It's rather fun, especially if they are knowledgeable," Sir Westrow Hulse, 9th baronet, says. "It took 20 years to catalogue the pictures alone." Retired village policeman, PC Crocker, became a guide.

In the old kitchen gardens, the Countryside Museum brings alive the life, transport and skills of bygone rural folk who — if they were local — were often surnamed Mouland, Witt, Mussell, Rooke, Hobbs, Dommett, Henstridge or Edsall.

Summer visitors may meet Breamore's Hayward of the Marsh, Hubert Henstridge in the church. He remembers the days of one bath a week and when you curtseyed in the street to The Honourable Lady Hulse. He began in the stables at Breamore House on nine shillings a week.

"It was really a thrill when the Wilton Foxhounds met on Boxing Day at Breamore. "Can I hold your horse, sir?" we'd ask, when the toffs went in for a glass of wine."

He still has old Charlie Dove's pig-sticking knife. "If you didn't hang your pig up your own chimney, one of the bakers would let you use his loft," he says.

Like the butcher, the baker came round with two or three freshly-baked loaves in a wicker basket, and the blacksmith carried his tools up to Breamore House.

In the Village Hall Mrs Cooper, the butler's wife, played the piano for the Sixpenny Hops, where you met the maids from the Big house.

Stern schoolmaster for 20 years, Mr Blunden also trained the choir. Lefthandedness was forbidden.

Today Edsalls blacksmith is still going strong . . . a family link with 1600. Breamore Stores and the Bat and Ball pub prosper and there's a dentist in the Methodist chapel. Only one flock of geese now lives on the Marsh, where once every tenant had rights.

Before 1651, about 300 people lived here. By 1851 there were 646. In 1985 it was only 334. For this, Breamore thanks the centuries under the benevolent Hulses.

"It's an unspoilt village . . . that's what I likes about it . . . Be good rabbits from Breamore Down."

Below: Historian and archeologist Anthony Light at Breamore Mill.

Blacksmith Trevor Kimber at work. His family have been Smiths in Breamore since the 15th century.

Vintage tractors are popular at the Breamore Countryside Museum.

Above: The Village Stocks pictured in 1974. They are now gone.

Below: Breamore Church.

Britford

LOWER BRITFORD seems impossibly rural. Only a mile from the city centre with the spire silhouetted against the sky, there are three working farms, water meadows still being flooded, thatched and creeper-covered garden walls and horses gently grazing.

"We're in the heart of the country, yet two steps from Salisbury," says Caroline Heaven at the trout farm where low-slung nets keep herons off. "It's a farming community."

True, the potholes in their gravel track are in the best rural tradition. Green droves still lead to Britford, though the sheep fair moved to Wilton.

But that's not the whole story. There's no smell of bread from the Old Bakery, where Winzer Gilbert's mother rendered down pig's fat for lardy cakes. The Old Forge is a gentleman's residence and so, too, is the Net House and Old Vicarage. There's a see-through central staircase in a newly-converted barn . . . and today Solento Cats are bred in the Cheese House.

Twentieth century horror is to be found on "the high road" (A338) where on the "deadly half-mile" 35 smashes have happened in 12 years . . . three were killed there in 13 months.

There, too, near the village hall, is Mrs Joy Cash's thriving school, built 1959, where the 79 children raise astonishing sums for charity (in 1986, Ethiopia got £1,000, NSPCC £400+, Barnardo's £168, NCH £116).

Only the parents' vigilance has prevented tragedy, says Mrs Cash. "On a wet day children arrive drenched with spray. The draught from the lorries terrifies me."

The Post Office closed in the 60s and there's no pub or shop. But there's still a splendid lock on the Christchurch to Salisbury canal for sailing barges (begun 1664) . . . and a moat with ducks and waterlilies.

Like Breamore, Britford's innocence was preserved by the reign of a single family (spelt Jervoise and pronounced Jarvis) from 1542 until July, 1962.

They preferred Herriard to Britford's castellated Moat House with its curly ("ogee-headed") windows. Since the sale, the absence of Deeds has given headaches to local solicitors.

The famous castellated Moat House with its 19th century ogee-headed windows.

Below: Mrs Boo Croysdill, a well-known feline fancier who breeds Solento cats at her home, The Cheese House.

Left: Children at the village school with the stamps they collected for Help the Aged in January 1987.

Right: The Radnor family Mausoleum behind the village church of St Peter.

Below: The old Britford ferry which was once rowed by Jack Mouland.

Below: Mark Heaven, owner of the Britford Trout Farm.

Sleepy Britford has its history; Peggy Shortt has dug it out. There was scandal, simony and daggers drawn in the churchyard in 1634, Sir George Pottersley locked the church against the clergy and a putrifying parson lay unburied for 12 days . . . when King Harold met Tostig here, Britford had 48 people . . . and to protect their privacy Eve of Presure and Joan of Britford, recluses, were walled up in 1237.

To begin, visit Britford's Paleolithic arrowhead and Neolithic handaxes in the Museum, make a detour towards Odstock hospital to Little Woodbury's Iron Age Farm and then go to church.

St Peter's is historic but chilly. Recycled Roman bricks were laid upside down by Saxons over the south arch. Opposite, a rare seventh-century craftsman carved delicate interlace patterns and scrolls enclosing grapes.

Solemn Shakespearean pilgrims visit the now-empty tomb of Henry, second Duke of Buckingham beheaded in Salisbury in 1483 by Richard III. And there's the great Radnor family mausoleum round the back.

Few grasp the hidden pun behind a tiny 1300 noseless figure lying on the windowsill in a pleated skirt, holding a covered cup. He's a man called Botelier (Butler). He died abroad, but thoughtfully sent home his heart.

I found narcissi on the grave of William George Clibbens Addison, Vicar 1939-1966, whose wife Lavinia remembers every detail of those years . . . from Lady Radnor in her wicker pony-drawn chair, to the terrible loos at the old school, stout Tom Hazel with pigswill in his trap, and the broad Wiltshire scolding she got on her tricycle from bent Winzer Gilbert.

The Moat House, vicarage and the house of Leonard Harris had electricity. He was "a great bellringer, who dug Jervoise ditches, cut hedges, and died cycling to Salisbury." Britford bellringers used to ring in the transept in their braces. James Lewis was another Britford campanologist. He died ringing at a wedding on the anniversary of his own.

"Once, when my husband was reading the lesson." Mrs Addison says, "he was aware of a sort of smile. Little mice were running down the bell ropes."

A sturdier rope was once suspended across the Avon . . . (and until Harnham built its bridge you HAD to cross at Britford or at Stratford). When Tom Hazel was a boy you paid a copper and used the rope to pull your boat across like a pontoon. Later, Jack Mouland rowed the ferry. His son still lives in Britford.

Harnham plague victims lie in Britford churchyard. So also do two ladies who had a punch-up in Salisbury Fair 1653 . . . the woman "slayne from a box on the ear" and the woman hanged for doing it.

By ancient right, if you live in Salisbury Close and want an old-fashioned burial, you must be buried at Britford. If you want your mortal remains to lie in the Close, you must be cremated.

Broad Chalke

CHURCH, pub, shop, school and village hall — picturesque Broad Chalke (1981 pop: 584) still has them all. It has been the chosen hideaway of at least one 20th century Prime Minister, Royal photographer and pop star. Cecil Beaton (photographer) and Christopher Wood (painter) are both buried in the churchyard.

There's mossy thatch in Broad Chalke, brick and flint and stone. The Ebble, crossed here and there by white-railed bridges, divides the village in two, and broadens out into Geoffrey Hitchings' watercress beds.

Its brass band has an international reputation. Here you can pick your own, drink quality coffee, aim high with your shotgun or try speed hill-climbing. To top it, a small hard-working nucleus provides a busy community life.

Little London (beloved by Sir Anthony Eden), Stoke Farthing, Bury Lane, Doves Meadow and the Knapp . . . storybook names, if you can find them. The local PTA is christened FOBS. No signboards on Manor Farm (where John Aubrey lived) or Reddish House (where Greta Garbo and Princess Margaret called) "We went by the names of people when I was postman," says Dennis Chalk.

At Mount Sorrell is Stephen Emm, haulage contractors (descendant of Henry Emm's carrier cart and bus service). On the other side of Broad Chalke is Ivor Smith's garage and the Bower Valley Gate and Fencing Supply.

South Street is the home of Fry family butcher's and the Whites at the busy Post Office. Their teashop is Egon Ronay-listed. They stock upmarket cheeses and Staffordshire snuff boxes, trout pâté and good coffee. "Anything from coal to exclusive Royal Yacht hairdressings," says Ian White.

Nearby is the village hall (red and gold velvet curtains a gift from Cecil Beaton), with its John Collier portrait of poet Maurice Hewlett who lived in King's Old Rectory.

The gallery of John Baker, equestrian artist, is close to the 1860 school. Nicknamed "Broad Chalke College" long ago by those who stayed to 14, today Broad Chalke First School has 40 five to nine year-olds.

Their sponsored spell raised £410 for the Spire. There's an illuminated model in the classroom. The children's written request for a follow-up to 'The Witches' provoked this doggerel from Roald Dahl, now framed nearby.

'As I grow old and just a trifle frayed, It's nice to know that I have sometimes made You children and occasionally the staff Stop work and have instead a little laugh.'

Above: The Emm bus service to Salisbury in 1928, with baby Stephen on the mudguard, Reginald at the wheel and Morgan leaning on the side of the 12-seater.

Left: Stephen Emm with the 1966 Scammell used as a breakdown truck for the Emm lorry fleet.

Opposite stands cruciform, crenellated All Saints church. Its 1740 gold clock (by William Monk, blacksmith of Berwick St John) overlooks the school, war memorial and the waiting mothers at the lychgate ('For the weary, rest').

The church dates from 1280 and the North Transept, Western Doorway and Chancel are largely original. But the ninth century fragment of a West Saxon preaching cross has earlier echoes.

It may have been at this cross that visiting friars preached in the open air long before Eadwy's charter of 955 gave Broad Chalke to the Abbess of Wilton or any church stood here.

On the sign outside the Queen's Head, a creeper reaches out its tendrils to Q. E's painted ruff. Bernard Lott and his wife Pamela bought Broad Chalke's freehouse this spring and Bernard's inn-keeping skills promptly won him a Brewers' Society silver medal.

"Broad Chalke ceased to be an agricultural village in the '50s," says Lieut-Col Godfrey Jeans. But on his estate there are still families like Chalk and Harris with astonishing long service records. The Gurds date back to Domesday.

Six substantial farms survive. ('Typical Wiltshire mixed farming'). Hugh Pickford at Stoke Farm has the last dairy herd, and at Knighton Manor Richard Lamb combines prizewinning pedigree Herefords and historical research.

Left: Champion gardener Mary Penny with her mother Florence in the garden of their Old Rafters home. Below: The village church of All Saints.

At Knapp Farm, David Hitching's shoot attracts international top 'guns' to enjoy the challenge of pheasants flying 30 to 40 yards high. Lunch is served in the fold of the downs and tea in the farmhouse overlooking his younger brother's startling green watercress beds.

At Gurston Farm Joan, Philip and Robert Hitchings have goats, arable farming and the celebrated RAC Speed Hill Climb. The 17th century pear tree Aubrey mentions has only just gone from Manor Farm.

Broad Chalke has its notable buildings. Reddish House, once home of Cecil Beaton, is a small 18th century brick manor house. King's Old Rectory has a splendid pre-Reformation archway and Elizabethan mullioned windows. Knighton Manor House has a 16th century doorway.

Thatched Yew Tree Farm is worth a second glance because, Monty Trethowan says, there lived Herbert Bundy, immortalised for winning his textbook lawcase against Lloyds Bank. A latter-day David and Goliath.

"OUR'S IS an interesting valley. We never had a railway. Elsewhere the political split was master and man, Conservative and Socialist. Here (as in North Dorset) radical Liberals opposed the Conservatives," says Lieut. Col. Godfrey Jeans, Broad Chalke's squire and Lord High Sheriff in 1985.

They nearly did have a railway. One was planned in 1899, says Monty Trethowan. His book tells Broad Chalke's story. You'll read of ploughing with a pointed stick, keeping roasted corn in pits, a Romano-British skeleton behind the Queen's Head in 1961 and the Saxon runrig system.

By 1384, he says, Broad Chalke had a mad chaplain and Edith Braunce (despite a gift of four ewes and two skeps of bees) gave the church no candles. During the Civil War, Major John Morgan (royalist) caught a malignant fever and was lodged secretly in a Broad Chalke "garett".

Today they still enjoy what Aubrey called the "tunablest ring of bells in Wiltshire." And a splendid collective memory. Flamboyant Cecil Beaton with his broad-brimmed straw hat, who had his hair cut by Dennis Chalk, "had a sweet mother" and invited the villagers in for champagne when he was knighted in 1972.

John Emm, aged 91 in the '20s ("looking like one of the seven dwarfs") delighted children with tales of the coaching days. "He'd seen the marks on the trees at Fifield where highwaymen were hanged."

"Every Sunday just before 11 opposite the butcher's I'd meet George Blick and his wife Annie in a long black dress and big hat off to chapel," says Stephen Emm, who still has his 1935 orange Sunday School Stamp Book.

The school outing was on St Swithin's Day. Mrs Moody who kept the sweetshop next to the thatched Malt House pub ("burnt down in '55") came down with

Above left: Lady Avon, then Clarissa Eden, the Prime Minister's wife, and the photographer Cecil Beaton at the village fete in 1955.

Top right: Dennis Chalk, B.E.M., former postman, conducts his Youth Band.

Right: Joe Ralls, the village bobby, on his Ariel motor-cycle combination, in 1934.

Bernard and Pamela Lotte, with dog Gipsy, outside their Queen's Head pub.

Broad Chalke Club Day 1897, celebrating Queen Victoria's Diamond Jubilee.

a basket of sweets.

"Dr Burroughs at Kings Old Rectory would take his chauffeur and maid back to Harley Street after tea on a Sunday. A big black car would appear through the archway and behind it a one-wheeled trailer of luggage."

Mrs Florence Penny was the daughter of a carter. She remembers old couples smoking their pipes together by the fire, men marching to church with their Slate Club banner and a First World War aeroplane landing at Gurston while she was home from school for lunch.

A framed testimonial tells how Flo cleaned All Saints Church for 42 years. Today its annual two-day spring clean, Gwen Hitchings says, involves 26 men and women in two-hour stints — dismantling, brushing, vinegar-and-watering woodwork and polishing.

In the days when the carrier would buy you everything from a stamp to a hairnet, you were scorched or frozen in school depending on where you sat, many families had ten or 12 children, TB and impetigo were rife and oil lamps were lit at the end of church pews.

"We boys turned the village bobby's bike upside down when he wasn't looking. But we respected him. I remember Sergeant Rose cuffing us round the ears for pinching apples — we daren't tell father or we'd have been thumped again."

"We would creep up to Gurston Farm where the cressing men were making their cider and blow out the candles in bottles."

"Cider making was an after-tea job lasting about ten days," says Stephen Emm. Everyone joined forces. The bitter-sweet apples were collected, cut up, ground and pressed in sacks. Sometimes the headlights of the old bus were used to supplement the candles.

Cider was enjoyed by all ages. "My grandparents would add loads of sugar and drink it at 9 at night heated by the fire with their onion, bread and cheese supper. But freshly-made it was very sweet."

Dr Woods pulled teeth for 6d in the back kitchen of Reddish House, Luke Barter's twice-yearly pantomimes were great innovations and Mrs Moon of the garage was unforgettable singing "My Old Man says Follow the Van."

Henry Poole, cobbler, wrote "Life in the Chalke village". He charged "6d if you please," for a screw, nail, or to charge wireless batteries.

"He soldered my first brass instrument," Dennis Chalk says. The first of many. His Wilton and District Youth Band has played for royalty, appeared on TV and been on many international tours.

"Playing in the band gives young people many things. On tour they learn how music-making brings people together. Between tours, they raise money for charity."

"Most people in the banding world don't give enough back to the young," says Dennis Chalk. His BEM was awarded for doing just that.

Pupils at the village school with their cardboard cathedral.

Coombe Bissett

TUCKED inconspicuously among the steep hills which enclose it, the village of Coombe Bissett is a close-knit community of 600 with a history stretching back 2,500 years.

That is why the children at Mrs Pat McKenzie's school on the hill built a thatched circular mud-walled hut in the playground among the climbing frames . . . an Iron Age house in the round.

Teaching techniques have changed since Mrs Nellie Farris suffered under the stern Joseph Drake, headteacher from 1888 to 1923.

"Girls were called 'Girl' and hit with a six-sided pencil that hurt like the devil. Once he broke his cane on a boy. You daren't blink, but we knew our 3Rs — and the scale drawing he taught was useful to many later on," she says.

Today the Ebbledown playgroup and Coombe Bissett school serve a wide catchment area, coaches bring visitors to the annual village pantomimes, the church is well attended, there's a cricket, badminton and embryonic tennis club, and a neighbourly spirit fostered by the parish magazine.

Its editor, Westley Cole, lives on a farm which overlooks the huddled village roofs.

"We still have the five essential ingredients — church, pub, shop, school and village hall," he says.

"Cumbe", he will tell you, belonged to the mother of unfortunate King Harold, before any Bysets arrived, though others will give you different explanations of the name.

He'll show you Saxon strip lynchets (which I mistook for terraces) an inaccurate turnpike milestone and a plague stone near the packhorse bridge where food was left out for victims of the Black Death.

Coombe Bissett boasted a brothel in 1408, a celebrated Farris steam plough foundry more recently, a gallows on Wick Down and its own Swing Riot in 1830.

The unhappy James Lush and George Toomer (two out of the 100) were singled out for transportation at the 1831 assizes. By the 1880s there was a village "Band of Hope," led by Canon Kingsbury.

Today Coombe Bissett is the home of many doctors and hospital consultants. Even in 1790 a doctor called Rose lived here. He undertook to nockelhead (meaning inoculate) "6 of the poore".

In St Michael and All Angels Church are further provisions for "the poore and aged" along with a mediaeval altar slab, priest's door and 1580 chest. An early airman is buried under a yew.

1987 saw the celebrations of the 900th birthday of the church, the 80th birthday of the well-loved rector, Rev Canon Percy Chapman, and the 50th anniversary of his ordination. He retired in 1988.

Artists live here today, Ray Evans and Tom Counter among them, but Mrs Farris will tell you how she saw the celebrated Henry Lamb visited by "Augustus John and his dreary bare-footed friends".

The village boasts an ADC to the Queen, retired soldiers and businessmen like Robert Bramwell ("Mr Village Hall"). Miss Florrie Farris helps run the village lottery, (they've raised £6,000 in five years . . . that's £10 a head). There are unseen benefactors too like the Thorne brothers who gave the village its recreation ground.

For 40 years Walt Mussell was a parish councillor. Today it is headed by Mrs Barbara Carter who has nineteenth-century roots in the village. It is, however, the Dyer family whom Westley Cole has traced back furthest — to 1575.

It was a Dyer; (one-legged Sid, who kept a talking magpie), who inherited Long Cottage, from the

Above: About 1900 a photographer snapped Nellie and friend in the old treadmill used to draw water from a deep well at her home.

Left: Today Mrs Nellie Farris at home with her dog Heidi.

Below: Wesley Cole by the "plague stone" near the pack horse bridge — it was probably a mounting block before the Black Death.

Above: A view of Coombe Bissett, which nestles in the valley of the River Ebble at the foot of the downs.

Below: The Band of Hope photographed in 1886 in the Vicarage garden. Canon Kingsbury is seated on the right.

famous Widow Ridout. Everyone knows about her donkey "Express" carrier service from Frank Brooks' 1875 painting "drawn walking slowly backwards."

Hospitable Maria Ridout not only gave ale to her donkeys at pubs to and from Salisbury but shared her inglenook fireplace with them.

Old Mrs Farris remembers generations of carriers, and a village where the blacksmith, Elias Lillington, was an important man because everyone had horses. He'd pay boys a penny for a horseshoe and the same for working the bellows.

She watched the fire of 1924 which destroyed five houses, and remembers her Mother's alarm when she rode in the first car in the village driven by "Hellfire Jack" (Lord Farquarharson of Blandford).

Now the lorries and commuters rush blindly down the Blandford Road where Nellie and her friends played with marbles and hoops. Water comes from taps not a donkey wheel.

But to the old timers of Coombe Bissett it is easy to close their eyes on Race Day, and remember how they gathered in front of the Fox and Goose pub to shout: "Off to the Races, Tally Ho; Give me a Penny before you Go!" And often got one, too.

Widow Ridout and the Coombe Bissett Express, the villagers' link with Salisbury.

Dinton

DINTON on the B3089 is a picturesque, friendly place. It has 485 people and 26 business large and small. Even its street names are quaint — Steep Hollow, Spracklands, Snow Hill and Bratch Lane.

It has a (sloping) village green for cricket and football with a 1981 pavilion ("Mothers and Toddlers Thursday mornings"), two churches and a chapel, two pubs, six National Trust houses, post office and red-brown "Victory" hall.

Until Monday, May 11, 1987 Dinton feared for its school. There were roadside placards in chalk, crayon and ink and mothers delivering children wore badges. But by noon Mrs Brenda Taylor's 28 pupils had won a reprieve. The OAPs will continue their Wednesday lunches with the children, the Mums their social afternoons and the children will swim in their pool this summer.

About 25 years ago, Dinton became smart and its cottages were done up. ("That's when we became a 'When We . . .' village," says Tony Bacon). You'll find it has a rest home but also an industrial estate, a vineyard, and a playschool.

Dinton has many claims to fame. Its long-serving post-mistress was invited to Buckingham Palace in 1984. Harold Wilson's son lives there and so did Baroness Evelyn Sharpe. The 1790 highwaywoman aged 24, Mary Sandall, came from tiny Baverstock and Dinton had a 19th century witch with 12 cats whose curses killed Mr Jukes.

Then there was Edward Hyde, first Earl of Clarendon who was Dinton-born (1608). He became Charles II's chancellor and grandfather to two queens — Mary and Anne.

Below St Edith's squat 14th tower in Baverstock hamlet are the neat white headstones of World War I flu victims — and a mass grave for 200 who died of Bubonic plague.

Until Henry VIII intervened, "Domnitone" or "Donynton" belonged to the Shaftesbury Benedictine nuns. Their 600-nest red-tiled stone dovecot at Hyde House is 12th century battery farming at its best.

In 1540 Dinton (worth £56 10s 11d) was given to Sir Thomas Arundel of Wardour who promptly lost his head. For 371 years, until 1918, the Pembrokes kept it. But they never owned Philipps House or its sweeping park.

That's where seven generations of Wyndhams lived. Designed by Jeffry Wyatt, it was once called Dinton House. Today few see its mighty central staircase lit from the dome above, its Victorian kitchens and its cellars stocked with Wyndham-crested bottles (empty). Up many flights of narrow wooden stairs are the attic servants' bedrooms, with windows blocked off. The "Young Gentlemen" had the use of bedrooms near the maids.

Above: The Wiltshire County Council Cheese School at Fitz Farm, Dinton, in 1912.

Right: The Roman Catholic church of Our Lady of Pity at Little Clarendon.

Below: The staff of five at Dinton Station in 1915.

Jim Gipson with Gladys, his wife and her mother, Ellen Townsend, when she was 99. St Mary's Parish church is in the background.

In the park, 2,000 Americans ("who were scared to walk through the graveyard") camped before D-Day and three (1/6d) dances a week were held in Victory Hall.

Until 1937, 40 worked at the brickfield with its 90ft chimney, (look in village wells for local bricks) and "at least 40 on the farms. Now, including bosses, there are eight."

Gone, too, are the famous annual pantomimes, flower show, tug o' war, band and Guy Fawkes parade and the "three double-deckers to Salisbury at 2 o'clock on Saturday."

Gordon Lake's grandfather was a Wyndham gamekeeper and his mother Hilda was a schoolma'am from 1919 to 1943. ("I was scared of her," says Tony Bacon).

Gladys Gipson's father, Vivian, was a Philipps gamekeeper — an "incredible marksman who wrote up his game book every day," says Group Capt John Smither, who keeps the village memories. Gladys grew up with an open range and a well, went ferreting, and walked a mile and a half to the oil-lit school.

Walter Clark, the wheelwright, was building wagons and Jimmy Baker at his forge when the children passed by, carrying milk home in a can with a push-in lid.

Dinton station closed in April, 1966. "It was full of activity, watercress from Fovant, sugar beet and passengers."

The American Nissan huts at Catherine Crescent were photographed before demolition on April 30, 1954. Gladys and her husband crept into an empty one at midnight to secure their first home. "It was soon a community of young mums, all having babies."

The hearse they once pushed from Teffont recently returned there. It is now on show at the Heavy Horse Centre.

Don't miss Little Clarendon (1460). Not just as the place where Rev G.H. Engleheart grew the first white daffodils . . . but "if you put a finger in the hole and lift the catch" you find yourself in the exquisite tiny RC chapel of Our Lady of Pity.

By contrast, the parish church is locked. The square 12th century font stands on little legs by the door. You'll find bell ropes in the transept, 14th century glass and George II's coat of arms high up.

Above The "squatters" from the old Dinton army huts move into the new council houses in 1954. Jim Gipson (centre) was the first "squatter". He worked at Dinton station. Now retired, still lives in the village with Gladys, his wife.

The Dinton Bonfire Boys, photographed towards the end of the 19th century, when the bonfire procession was a major annual event.

Downton

ONLY 2,810 people live in Downton yet everyone from King John to primary schoolchildren on the Downton Project seems to have heard of it.

After all, Princess Diana's wedding garter and Princess Margaret's bridal hanky were made from Downton lace, Downton Engineering made Minis into racers, its agricultural college rivalled Cirencester and the Kodak Eastman family sprang from there.

So did the first picture bought by the National Gallery. It features Sir Walter Raleigh . . . and maybe Queen Elizabeth I suspected it might someday fill 150 pages of the Victoria History. Certainly she suddenly decided in 1586 to have lunch in Downton at the Manor House she had confiscated for Raleigh.

The story goes that he sailed a barge up the Avon and inverted the keel to support the roof. "I've seen it", says JP Peter Waddington. "It's still there."

People have been attracted to Downton for 6,000 years, first for its river crossing and today for its community life. Mesolithic, Neolithic and Beaker remains were found in 1955 on the Avon river terraces.

In 1952, an unsuspecting Mr Churchill decided to put up a washing line near Moot Lane and revealed the pavement of a 17-room Roman Villa built 300 AD.

Saxons and Normans moved northwards along the valley to the church and High Street. By Domesday, Downton belonged to the Bishop of Winchester and Winchester College is still the Patron of St Lawrence's. To find the church you have to seek it out, turning away from the thatched High Street cottages.

The church is large and well kept. I was impressed, and not only by the Scheemakers Georgian monuments or the good-tempered tower which Lord Radnor raised to improve his view in 1791. (It was lowered in 1860).

A 1743 stone in the outside wall remembers Will Kervil (32), servant to Anthony Duncombe. "Judge of his character by the general regret of his Fellow Servents and by this Testimony of his Affectionate Master and Lady's regard for his faithful, diligent and cheerful service during the space of 21 years."

The Borough, broad street with manicured lawns, was built in 1205 as a New Town to provide cash revenue instead of feudal dues for Winchester. The boundary stone can be seen in the wall of Borough Manor (1673). Lord Radnor numbered the house fronts.

Each Burgage of this "Rotten Borough" had until the Reform Act a parliamentary vote. The two MPs were proclaimed from the Borough Cross (with its handy whipping stone thoughtfully placed beside it). Downton's mayor Hobbs also lost his job in 1833 but refused to surrender his mace.

The dilapidated temple in the Moot grounds in 1975.

Below: The old Corn Store and Bacon Factory, once the workhouse, recently became a chemical pipe factory.

Above: Up to their axles! The floods of 1954.

Left: Alfred "Stubby" Sherwood started his working life on the land and ended as caretaker of Downton Junior school.

Newcourt Farm has impressive late 17th century buildings, the pubs are notable and so is the Old Workhouse (1730) which has progressed from the destitute to making gloves, carpets, bacon and Chemical Plastic Pipes and Vessels.

Members of Downton Society are concerned with the present as well as the past. But it took them ten memorable years under Charles Greville-Heygate, to achieve public ownership of the Moot (= Motte).

This Norman castle mound, once supposed a Saxon meeting place, in the celebrated 18th century landscaped garden of Moot House ("a Queen Anne country gentleman's residence") fell into dilapidation in the hands of Mike Kemmis, Channel Islands-based developer.

Trafalgar House with its Nelson family link is nearby. Lady Nelson drove over from Standlynch to open the railway station.

Opposite the modern Tannery (built 1919) are two old mills — one a grist mill and hydro-electric station. The other made paper until 1920.

In the 19th century Downton was in its agricultural heyday and a village of many trades. There was a basket-maker, butcher, cooper, draper, joiner carpenter, dressmaker, blacksmith, brewer, tailor and (of course) lacemaker.

But today, only six miles from Salisbury's chain-stores, surely Downton is well-served by Mr Bailey's wet fish, four grocers, two banks, two Post Offices, five pubs, newsagent, haberdashery, chemist, optician, dentist, vet and industrial estate.

So don't believe the refrain you hear: "We are losing all our shops."

The younger Dr Brian Whitehead (seated, wearing top hat) enjoying a rest outside the White Horse during a round-the-village wheelbarrow race in the 1950s.

THERE was never any rain at harvest time. We never took a jacket, says Alfred ("Stubby") Sherwood, recalling his Downton boyhood nearly 80 years later.

Only in his last year at Newcourt Farm, where at 14 he had taken the place of a sick stable lad, did the climate alter.

"The corn became big heaps of manure. We couldn't get it in." Those were the days when the corn was cut, tied, opened and stacked in ricks. Today only thatchers do it that way he says.

Agricultural Downton lasted a long time. "There's nothing like farm work. It's a 1,000 pities everybody now is out for a fast buck. We were close to nature and wanted nothing more."

Now four men do the work of 30 and none start the day as Stubby did, taking out horses for waggoning at 6.30 am. Nor, end up pinned to the ground under a plough because they weigh too little.

He was actually sacked while ploughing.

"The wheel came off my plough, so off I went to the hedge for a piece of wood to fix it on. Up rode Bob Reid on his big chestnut horse, and found me stopped, mending the plough. 'You be off,' he said, so I took him at his word and left it all in mid-field."

Stubby, who rose to be chairman of the parish council (and seemingly of nearly every village society) remembers as a boy scrabbling for toffees thrown into the air by Mr Warren during the Baptist Chapel wagon outing.

But a bigger drama happened in the candlelit January days of 1915 — a flood so great "we kept both doors open to keep the water running". Boats sailed down the borough. Neighbours visited by climbing on the backs of chairs and Nadder Mussell fell in when his chair broke.

Gardening was a school subject in long-ago Downton and you could keep your produce. Even Stubby's labourer father who worked a six-day week had time and energy to keep an allotment. His mother took in washing.

A remarkable chemist, early photographer, supplier of Avonvale mineral water and a famous sheep dip was C. H. Dunmore. He lived for 50 years beside today's Lloyds bank. He left hundreds of glass plates which give us a pictorial record of Downton in his day.

Apparently the last public appearance of the Downton mace.

Above: Daphne Greville-Heygate with her pony Tamud.

Left: The Green in 1924, (less manicured than in 1988.)

Top: The ancient Downton cross in The Borough.

Above: Steppin' Out — The Dance Group that grew and grew!

Earlier relics — medieval leather shoes — appeared recently inside a chimney in the borough. They had been hung there for good fortune long ago.

The first of the three generations of Whitehead doctors came to Downton in 1919 when the new tannery was built. Gas lamplighters had gone but village boys still went rabbiting and fishing for eels. Daphne Greville-Heygate was his daughter. She remembers cleaning bottles and letting in patients at Hamilton House.

"Old Mr Gwyr came rubbish-collecting with his carthorse," she says. Poor Dummy Cooper was run over. Her jobs included the fire in the wooden-seated waiting room and fetching milk from Parsonage Farm (where Raleigh stayed).

Gypsies came in early spring to sell wild snowdrops set in pine cones. Later in the year they brought split-wood flowers.

Her brother, the Brian Whitehead honoured in the Sports Centre, is fondly remembered everywhere ("He was a beautiful chap . . . He mixed with the people . . . Dr Miranda is still here").

He was carnival chairman, keen on dramatics like his father and started Eventide and the old people's outings. Good Companions began, Ruth Holman says, "because the sight of three old men walking each day with nowhere to sit and rest made me wish for a club for the lonely and not-so-young". There is also the successful Barford Day Centre in St Lawrence's Hall.

Mrs Ethel Gray (born Stevens) lived at Load Hill near Downton station when the terrible (June 3, 1894) Downton rail crash occurred at Pile Bridge. She remembers how the 4.50 Salisbury-Wimborne market-day train was derailed at 70 mph.

Five died and 41 were injured as the train plunged 12 foot into a "watery ditch". Bodies were laid out on the bank and Queen Victoria sent a telegram to the Infirmary to know how the "poor sufferers" from the Downton accident were progressing.

Indigenous Downtonians like Bert Blake, Jack Bailey (of the Band), Ted Gunston, Percy Newman and Cocky Kingshot took the railway for granted until it closed in 1964. Today it is remembered only in street names.

It was a patient of Dr Whitehead's who predicted a personal Downton station visit from the King and Queen during their 1943 Southern tour before D-Day.

"How do you know?" asked the good doctor, for security was tight. "They've just washed the waiting room floor," came the reply, "for the first time since it was built."

Sure enough, little Daphne Whitehead and many others watched George VI and his Queen get aboard and steam away with their two little girls at the window.

DOWNTON'S got everything, I was told, the river, the downs, the forest, the sea, Salisbury and Southampton. " We very seldom leave the village for pleasure . . ."

"Our second Sunday family service attracts up to 300. Our rector wrote it himself. It's not matins in disguise."

St Lawrence's is linked with a Pakistani church. It has successfully insulated its roof, carpeted and decorated itself, reclaimed its churchyard (with the Burnbake Trust) and rebuilt its venerable organ.

Its pantomime, which raised £500 this year, gets everyone together. In May, 1983, it spawned Linda Crocker's successful "Stepping Out" dance studio which has now 170 pupils.

Baptists, Methodists and Catholics join Lent Study groups. But the event which really brings the crowds to the green lawns of the Borough is the 600-year-old Cuckoo Fair, which stopped during World War I and was revived seven years ago.

"We wanted to recapture its spirit," says Peter Waddington. "Picture them long ago. They'd seen no friends all winter, they'd make things to sell. They'd buy and sell animals, visit inns and find work."

Today there are 220 stalls, two marquees and street entertainers. There's band playing (Downton's Huntsman band is famous) and dancing round the Maypole. Apart from the fun of the Punch and Judy, Tea and Football dances, it's a chance for local fund-raising.

In Downton there's a lot on — from two WIs (market Friday) to Playgroup, clubs ranging from Tennis to Pandas, anything from the esoteric to Scouts. Somehow Jack Miles found time to make a garden out of crockery.

Incredibly, they used to do more. Old bound parish magazines tell of three-day church fetes with fireworks nightly in Moot gardens. In those days St Lawrence's lent out blankets in winter.

It's not all play in modern Downton. They boast two "excellent" state schools — the secondary one which opened in May, 1965, also caters for wheelchair pupils.

"No one wants this academically sound, caring school to be swallowed up in any future reorganisation," says Biddy Carr, once Senior Mistress.

There's currently a plea for help with two goats at the Rural Studies centre. The newsletter of the Downton Project (began September, 1985) tells of exciting primary school opportunities.

Downton is fortunate in having local employment — including the ever-expanding Colourcare laboratory which employs 200 of its workforce of 1,800 in Downton.

The Downton Tanning Company, since 1962 under Andrew Lunt, still processes hides as it has for centuries, but nowadays mainly for harnessware and belting. One of the last six British tanneries left, they employ 60.

Then there's Fitch and Son, wholesale caterers, employing 80, Hydor Air Conditioning, Mitchells Timber Yard, light engineering (various), Printing, and Chemical Plastic Pipes and Vessels in the Workhouse.

The population ranges "from near-county to the indigenous salt of the earth", numbering 1,352 in 1931 and 2,786 by 1981. The new estates brought new talents and ratepayers, but also an increase in vandalism. "Even the cricket pavilion got burnt."

The whole community united in a campaign for a school crossing after the death of Janine Thomason in October, 1986. But they rejected a recent plan for a bypass linked to high density development. "Though we need the cheap housing, we want to remain a large village. That would have turned us into a town,' the Downton villagers defiantly say.

Downton's latest PC, Paul Cripps, who arrived on February 11, 1987, in time to play PC Pong in the pantomime, has a different style from his 1920s predecessor "Gasher" Waite ("a big stout chap, he was, in his glory in a fight". He chucked out troublemakers from the 2/6d dances one under each arm).

The new bobby has the care of an energetic and heterogeneous population, in an extraordinary fish-shaped parish, criss-crossed with bridleways and footpaths which men have used for 6,000 years.

Top: A 1971 aerial view of the east end of Downton, showing the Tannery and the Moot.

Above: The Downton Huntsman Band leading the Cuckoo Fair procession through the village.

Right: Life-long Downtonian Ted Gunston (left) enjoys a game of cards with Leslie Pearce at the Barford Day Centre in St Laurence's Hall.

Durrington

Top: The Cross Stones, as old as Stonehenge, with the Old Rectory in the background.

Above: Flashback to 1910 . . . children playing around the Stones before the Cross was added.

Below: Woodhenge today has six concentric rings of concrete pillars. They mark the position of the supporting wooden posts of a long-lost round timber building.

DURRINGTON is not a pretentious village, though it has much to boast about. For within its parish boundaries lie some of our most ancient national monuments.

Ask today's villagers about Durrington Walls, and many of them think of the telephone exchange — not the mighty oval bank and ditch enclosing 4,000-year-old circular sacred buildings which were excavated in a hurry in 1966.

"I used to go up there every day," Herbert Richardson recalls. "Do you realise the ditch took a million man hours to complete? And it was all done with deer antler picks and shoulder blade shovels."

He remembers every detail of Dr C. J. Wainwright's dig. "The college undergraduates camped on the bank opposite Woodhenge.

"The post holes were huge — trees then must have been enormous. You could see the different layers, even the silt from a prehistoric flood."

Mr Richardson even brought home some prehistoric topsoil and put it in his greenhouse — but no prehistoric plants grew.

It was not the widening of a road, but circles spotted from the air which pinpointed Woodhenge. In 1925 Squadron Leader Insall photographed white chalk marks forming a circle in a field of young wheat.

The dig which followed showed Woodhenge was a wooden prototype for Stonehenge, with a three-year-old child sacrificed in the middle. Its skull was cleft.

A "Beaker" youth with a brain cavity far larger than ours was buried in the outer ditch. As at Stonehenge, compass and solstice calculations were exact.

Right in the heart of Durrington stand some stones as old as Stonehenge. Since 1919 they have been topped by the War Memorial cross, but their origins are, like the nearby flint mines, lost in prehistory.

The earliest written records tell of "Derintone's" taxes at the time of Edward the Confessor, when the village was bounded by gates to keep out "beasts" and strong ale kept serfs cheerful.

William the Conqueror gave Derintone intact to a Norman, Alberic de Vere, but it was to split. East End passed to the Dean of Sarum in 1207 and he kept it for 650 years.

West End Manor became Durrington Manor. Nearly 1,000 years later there is a fine house by that name overlooking Hackthorne and the tranquil Avon.

In 1398, William of Wykeham bought "Durenton Manor" for Winchester College. He paid £1,066 13s 4d which went towards the costs of building Manchester Cathedral. It was Winchester's for 500 years and there is still a College Road.

Henry VIII took the "Capella de Durenton" from Amesbury convent and gave it to the Dean and Chapter of Winchester. They are still patrons of the parish church.

In 1549, Robert Matyn bequeathed a cow to maintain "a lampe before the Blessed Sacrament . . . the which Kow I will that oon of my kynred have in keping to the behalf of the said lampe and the parisshe to set him from man to man soo that the kow never dye".

I could find no sign of that perpetual cow in the fine Church of All Saints with its knapped flints and rediscovered Norman entrance arch.

But there is a touching little 1633 brass to "the immature death of deare brother Iohn Poore" who died aged three and the Jacobean carving of pews and pulpit are exquisite.

The most recent innovations have created a central platform to bring the priest into the congregation.

There is a new west door and a draught-proof porch and the Rev Kenneth Batt "feels privileged to serve here."

"I feel at home here. They are my kind of people. They are open, warm-hearted, willing and dedicated to making this community alive."

Among his predecessors were 1456 chaplain John Mareys, who witnessed St Osmund's miracles and Richard Webb, who gave up the glebe and vicarage to found the first school in 1843. Then there was the powerful Charles Snelling Ruddle (rector 1863-1910), who wrote a village history.

"I remember Canon Aubrey Ruddle, his son," says Mrs Edna Richardson, "very large and majestic in his cassock and cloak. You'd be careful not to misbehave and the boys would touch their hands to their hats as he passed."

Durrington today is a far cry from the 1676 hamlet of 334 people. As in 1704, there are still Batchelors and Smiths (yeomen), Rangers and Spreadburys. Toomer and Sturgess are also Durrington names.

In 1801 there were 339 living here; in 1901, 434. But by 1951 the population included Larkhill and was 5,784 and in 1981 6,746. There are more houses to come.

The 20th century has turned Durrington into a rural commuter belt . . . a sprawling civilian parish in a massive military area. And it has a vibrant village life.

Flashback to the 1960s . . . Rangers Corner Garage, Hillman dealers.

"THEY'VE got a big heart in Durrington, if you can catch them in," former newsagent Dick Steadman told me. "They've paid for 14 guide dogs."

He showed me round the Day Centre where Durrington's elderly happily spend their Fridays.

There was 92-year-old Florence Keel, ready to tell me about school in 1897 and housemaid training in Swanage. Durrington's air must be bracing.

It boasts three churches, four hairdressers, two estate agents, two pubs, three takeaways, two grocers, a hardware store, photographer, baker and post office.

"If only people would shop here, it would be perfect," I was told. "A central shopping area would have given the village a heart."

But, as Herbert Richardson explains, houses were top priority after the war . . . people lived in leaking Nissen huts, cold, with no privacy.

"We got in as many houses as we could and even kept the roads narrow to keep costs down."

There are two doctors, but no dentist, chemist or vet. And bus fares to Salisbury and Amesbury are steep. A pity, for by and large, Durrington is not an affluent village.

It is certainly an energetic one. Local entrepreneurs abound. From Carton Industries, Rangers Garage (which began with the first village charabanc) to upholstery, snooker, ice-cream and painting.

The Defence Land Agency is still impressive but no-one there has the reputation of Colonel and Mrs Piggott in the '30s.

Top: A bird's eye view looking towards Bulford, with the Stonehenge Inn visible near the roundabout.

Above: A float in a Durrington Carnival of long ago.

Below: Class 3 in 1933 at Durrington Junior School (the present Infants' School) in School Road. At least 12 of the pupils still live nearby, including Mrs Joyce Smith (blond girl seated centre) and Terry Heffernan (far left with crossed legs).

The Rev Kenneth Batt, rector, inside All Saints' Parish Church.

A born-and-bred villager, Mrs Joyce Smith, in her husband's butcher's shop in 1987.

A Romano-British kiln uncovered near Larkhill in 1971.

"She was village Lady Bountiful," recalls Terry Heffernan. "She ran the choir and the Conservative Association," says Edna Richardson.

Durrington Corps of Drums has made its name, but there is everything from the WI and patchwork to drama, whist, badminton and football.

At the big comprehensive school, Roger Clay seeks to establish a community centre for the Upper Avon Valley. His 850 pupils, he points out, only use the valuable site 190 days a year.

Like the other headteachers, Neil Ruck and Sheila Laughton, he encourages parents' visits. He also brings staff out to nine villages for evening consultations each term.

Durrington is proud of its parish hall — built with a controversial 2p on the rates and "booked solid".

The pretty old cottages are down near the Avon and Hackthorne, where Mr McCann saw the Cavalier ghost.

"He was a down-to-earth man," says Herbert Richardson, "and he was off to post a letter when he felt a sudden cold shiver. He looked up and saw the back view of a cavalier near the cross stones. Shattered, he went to see Canon Ruddle.

'You are privileged,' the rector told him. 'Records tell of a cavalier resting down at Hackthorne who was killed by Roundheads while his horse was being shod. Periodically he walks back up for his horse.' "

There are a few left who recall the days when Larkhill was downland. There in tents Canadians and Australians (whose graves are in Hackthorne cemetery) died of 'flu and spotted fever.

They remember Mrs Smith's shop "where you got sweets in three-cornered bags and ate them in the pungent smell of the smithy."

Meads Road was a track when they rode in a haywagon, clinging to the ladder at the back . . . "I used to run behind the reaper and binder to hit the rats with my stick," says another.

There was fishing for gudgeon, stickleback and crayfish in the Avon, birdnesting and scrumping for apples on the way home from school . . .

Infant teacher Mrs Dowsett pulled out milk teeth with a clean hanky . . .

After harvesting, the henhouse on wheels was towed by horse to the cornfield, "free range" hens competing with old ladies for the gleanings . . .

Today it is hard to believe there were once no keys for the doors. Petty crime came with the big new settlements.

Few now know the nicknames for every stretch of the road to Salisbury, but they have retained the community feelings of an old-fashioned village.

As I was talking in the late-lamented Butcher's shop, in came someone. "There's a burst pipe down the road, so I told them, just go and tell the butcher's wife. She'll see to it."

I wouldn't live anywhere else," says Mrs Joyce Smith. "Have you seen the new Catholic church? We are a lucky village.

"Our carnival brings the whole village together." Until 1900, the May 13 maypole at the cross stones united them in the same way. Plus ça change . . .

Farley

THE SQUEAL of astonished tyres is often heard in the tiny village of Farley (99 houses, muddy lanes forming a circle, forest all round).

Nothing prepares the unsuspecting visitor for what is round that corner. He has passed unremarkable bungalows and occasional thatch, the post office, the pub, a thatched cob wall, the 1868 ("excellent") school, a vivid green Reading Room and suddenly, there it is — the architectural elegance of 17th century London.

Farley's glory is her church and almshouses, gift of her greatest son. Sir Stephen Fox paid for them, Alexander Fort built them, Sir Christopher Wren may even have drawn the plans — but the bricks were made locally at Grub Ground, near Knightswood.

Fox, son of a Farley yeoman, had a meteoric career. Whether he concealed Charles II by plunging him into a pond or setting him to hurdlemaking (both stories have local advocates), he certainly followed him to France and became his Paymaster General and Keeper of the Privy Purse.

He kept his integrity. He founded the Chelsea Hospital for Disabled Soldiers and secretly endowed Salisbury Cathedral School. His energies were prodigious. His 14 children included Charles James Fox, Stephen, later Lord Ilchester and Henry, Lord Holland. And of course, he's buried in Farley.

First came the 1681 sheltered housing scheme for 12. All Saints church followed in 1688. "Fox said people needed somewhere to live before they needed somewhere to pray," says Pearl Bray. She loves her one-up-one-down almshouse.

In the middle under a Latin plaque is the wardenry, intended as a school, used until 1981 as a vicarage and now family home to consultant Richard Godfrey, warden.

Some 1683 regulations have been relaxed. No more prayers twice daily or sermons from the warden. But Lely's portrait of Fox still dominates the parlour, and every year Richard fills in one page in the great padlocked account book which Fox began.

Farley has its controversies. The Farley twice mentioned in Domesday lies elsewhere, says Michael Parsons. Colt Hoare read it differently. From FARLEGE (worth 70 shillings) it became Fernelega in 1109, Fernlee (1185), Ferleg (1198) and Farley Juxta Pitton in 1285.

They say the pub is unique. Not for cribbage or quizzes, visits from a poet laureate or newlaid eggs . . . but for its name, the Hook and Glove. (Is there really another in Shropshire?).

Reapers used a riphook and hedgers used a glove. But Farley folk believe their Hook and Glove are hurdlemakers' tools. For Farley woodmen were famous. Their fenders, faggots and fascines travelled the country. ("And Chunky Parsons still makes hurdles.")

Parsons, Williams, Battens, Brays, Foxes, Frys and Pragnells still live in Farley. They have a proud heritage. In 1901 J.W. Garton's ill-advised gamekeeper blocked the footpaths to Salisbury across Clarendon Estate. Fisticuffs followed and "Mr E. Pragnell smashed the chains".

Though most of them had never seen a train before, 50 village stalwarts set off by rail to fight the 1903 case in Devizes. Two of the three footpaths were saved.

Pearl Bray knew Farley in 1920. Newspapers came with the milk from Dean station and she delivered them. One old man would mend her punctures if she'd read to him. She'd meet Mr Coward taking his cow for a walk on a lead. Worms wriggled in the well water even after you'd boiled it, and "I did pity the poor bear that came with the organ."

David "Chunky" Parsons, Farley's last sparmaker, seen at work cutting the hazel in his wood shed at Farley Farm cottage.

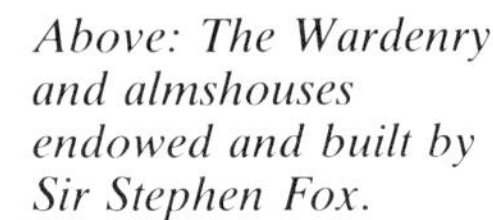

Above: The Wardenry and almshouses endowed and built by Sir Stephen Fox.

Left: An engraving of Sir Christopher Wren on the window of Miss Pearl Bray's home in the Almshouses. Sir Stephen Fox's face is engraved on a lower pane.

Three-hundred-year-old All Saints Church, built by Sir Stephen Fox to designs by Sir Christopher Wren.

Right: The champions who fought for the Rights of Way from Farley and Pitton through Clarendon to Salisbury in 1901 to 1903.

Below: Licensee Chris Morgan and his wife Gill under the controversial Hook and Glove pub sign.

They don't any longer show "unspeakable movies" (Mary Walker's phrase) in the Reading Room, but it doubles as Village Hall, extra classroom and dining hall. There's drama, Friday Sunday School, Keep Fit and Brownies. Pam Henry from the Post Office runs the Beavers and there's a fete in June on the four-acre playing field.

"It's a good village. They muscle in." They built their own cricket pavilion. (It was outsiders who burned it down.) Marjorie Stagg raises money for Farley Ward, polio victim Elizabeth Fanshaw won an OBE for her work for the disabled, Patrick Crozier-Cole and Dr Godfrey found, moved and built the church organ. There's even a Farley festival.

Farley pride really surfaced when the church celebrated its 300th birthday.

The tale goes that in 1688, Farley was overjoyed with its new church. Not because of Wren's renown. Nor because the old one had been wooden. But theirs was bigger than Pitton's. They'd been relegated to the paupers' pews, there.

The Americans have copied Farley church. It's Christ Church, Lancaster, Co. Virginia built by wealthy planter, Robert "King" Carter in 1732.

Though they may have a better bus service, they haven't an almshouse or a buried Roman villa in Virginia. There are no tales of Belgian refugees either, and no-one there remembers Tyker Yeates, poacher ('who needed two policemen to catch him").

Figheldean

PICTURESQUE Figheldean beside the Avon is like a family. It is full of private allusions. Everyone's proud of Mrs Seabrook's longevity. Reg's Boots, they say, will appear on the new church wallhanging.

"We could hear Rev Stratton smile up the road." Remember "Knuckle" Sheppard, the roadman? He was always refilling his pipe and could find you mushrooms. "Lisha" Carter collected nightsoil on a handcart. "You knew when he'd been . . ."

In a leaking two-bedroomed thatched cottage there lived a widow, four daughters, two sons, a lodger, Frizzie and Twerp ("who died from a bath").

Here, obviously, change comes slowly. For more than 1000 years, Figheldean has kept its Danish name. It means Valley of the Birds.

Under Longfellow's Spreading Chestnut Tree (one of 11 UK "originals") stands the famous Smithy with a mossy roof. Motionless, noseless, in the church porch, feet crossed on their dogs, lie two 13th century knights. There's even an original Daguerrotype in the rose above the South Chancel window.

In 1880 the population was 456. That year Figheldean had Longfellow's smith complete with brawny arms and sinewy hands, seven large farms, a lord of the manor, a vicar, three large houses, a parish clerk, carpenter, wheelwright, shoemaker, machinist, baker and storekeeper.

Today its population is 672. Leaving Alton Magna Farmhouse on your right, cross the bridge, pass the redbrick 500-member Working Man's Club and the yellowbrick 1958 village school (54 local children under headmaster Tim Coles).

Thatch and flint cottages appear. Signs like Pollen Lane and Goat's Milk for Sale. A Post Office shop. Beyond the whitewalled Wheatsheaf (where the King of Siam once drank) they're thatching with golden straw and Norfolk reed. The meat packing factory is less romantic.

In the heart of the village is the "market square". There they played football till the copper took the ball. Today you find breathtaking cottage gardens and Figheldean House, official residence of Larkhill Camp's Commandant.

The MOD encircles (and largely employs) the village. It owns the farms and thatched Ablington where the houses are numbered haphazardly as the government bought them. The riverbank and its fishing are out of bounds. They belong to a servicemen's fishing club.

Below: Coronation celebrations in Figheldean in 1953.

Below: Figheldean Mill — the landmark that disappeared.

Below: Eric Hill holds his old village postcards (shown left) which capture the quiet charm of bygone Figheldean.

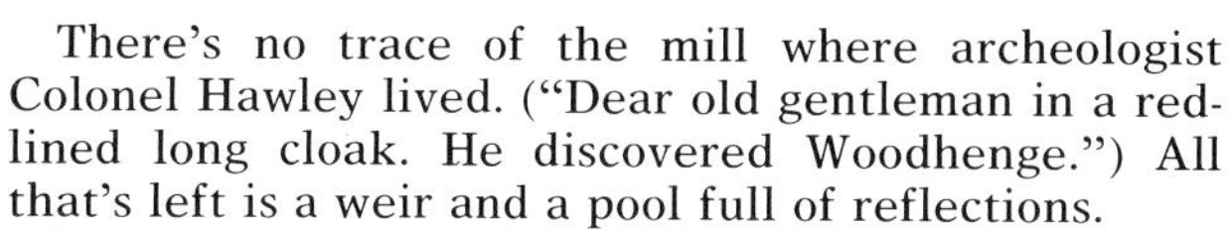

There's no trace of the mill where archeologist Colonel Hawley lived. ("Dear old gentleman in a red-lined long cloak. He discovered Woodhenge.") All that's left is a weir and a pool full of reflections.

Den Sawyer was born in the mill. "There was a light but it wasn't safe." So they used oil lamps and his uncle carried water down with a yoke. On the lawns of Figheldean House, the Mother's Union was making camouflage nets. As a wartime child, he earned chocolate bars carrying parachutes, and picked nettles, rosehips and burdock leaves for the Red Cross.

Eric Hill, Working Man's Club trustee for 35 years, was born in 1913. He walked five miles to school from Syrencot Pennings on the Plain, often hiding behind the hayricks or lambing hurdles to get warm.

They would lead horses at harvest time and clean officers' buttons. After school, they used a pillowcase to carry home the bread.

His mother raised ten children and took in army washing, but wasn't too busy to take blankets to crashed airmen.

Mrs Rawlings, longtime farmer, remembers "bathwater running down the road." One house at Milston, she says, was "all barbed wire" when they

Above right: Den Sawyer, who was born in the vanished mill, in his well-kept garden.

planned the D-Day landings. The King and Queen stayed at Syrencot when the first airborne division was formed. The floods of October 27 1960 made water come out of the pump unbidden.

Today, the Methodist Chapel has closed and the parish hall is a little wan. But the Church of St Michael is well supported and warmed by new short-wave infra-red heating. There's Sunday school on Mondays. Kirsten Slater's inspiration and 50 needleworkers have produced more than 100 tapestry kneelers showing the birds of the valley.

In this church graced by memorials to Salisbury's celebrated Poores and the crusader flogged twice in his nether garments, Rev David Slater will "toss a pancake or don national costume and dance." His parishioners are delighted.

Opposite the church lives Len Mousley, 34 years parish council chairman. Today, he keeps Figheldean's flag and Jubilee film. He has presided over historic debates on sewerage and street lights, council houses and playing fields — innovations in the 50 years since each house got "three lights and a plug".

Now there are Meals on Wheels, Brownies and Keep Fit, flower arranging, whist, Figheldean Singers and Over '60s. The blacksmith packed up his anvil in 1938. The carol singers no longer use lanterns and have to take out insurance. October half-term isn't Spud-Picking holiday.

So things have changed (if slowly) in Figheldean, which was called Fisgledene in Domesday, Figgledon in 1666 and Filedon in 1718.

Fordingbridge

FORDINGBRIDGE today is a country town of 5380, discovering a new pride in itself. A recent TV programme spotlighted this. Local residents are talking about it. ("It's coming back. Do you remember the old Regatta days?")

It goes further than hanging baskets, window boxes and the revival of the annual carnival. Or the plan for a tapestry of the town photographed from the air.

There's the agitation over the future of Avonway — the school turned community centre, where 38 clubs meet ("toddlers to centenarians").

The dynamic new Fordingbridge Society continues fighting the pollution of the River Avon, government inquiry notwithstanding. They're rehabilitating the neglected grave and bronze statue of Augustus John (he's to be moved to the new library) and crusading against the gravel lorries in its bottleneck High Street.

It couldn't stop the demise of Ferndown House — its timbers and bricks were sold piecemeal. But the boarded-up Greyhound Inn may have a brighter future. Likewise the home of the Hyde Band, the red-brick Victoria Rooms over the bridge at Horseport, given to the town in a 1874 Trust by Thomas Westlake "for social and educational purposes."

Fordingbridge is waking up to tourists. A Welcome to Fordingbridge leaflet ("Where the Chase meets the Forest") is to be found everywhere. There's a shopper's guide, too.

At Sandy Balls (the name, from 1490, is geological, not biological) is the successful Westlake family holiday centre which attracts 2500 summer visitors a week. In the deep shade of its forest trees, log cabins house everything caravanners want, from the indoor swimming pool with sauna, to launderette, shop and games room.

For trippers there are trinkets, coffee shops and takeaways (Indian, Chinese, Fish and Chips). There's still old-world courtesy in the air. People stand and chat. More important, it's a real shopping centre. ("Search Salisbury and find it in Fordingbridge", they told me.)

In recent years, quiet Fordingbridge has seen improbable dramas the town would prefer to forget, though no-one can forget the Burgate massacre. But most of the headlines were about the Roundhill car park, the twinning with Vimoutiers on the river

John Barron, retired plastic surgeon, with the controversial statue of his controversial friend, "Augustus John, O.M., R.A.". The statue of the artist who lived at Fryern Court, by Ivor Robert-Jones is shortly to be moved from the "Rec" to the new library.

Orne, Normandy, the new fire engine, the business-women's luncheon club and the library petition. For that is the real stuff of country town life.

Here is the national headquarters of the Game Conservancy. Patients at the 74-bed Infirmary enjoy the summer sunshine. (High above is the belfry erected in 1887, when this "large and commodious" Union Workhouse was built.) There's a splendid recreation ground beside the Avon (beloved of the Turks Football Club) and, of course, doctors, dentists, vets, nursing homes and churches.

The light, modern Catholic Church of St Mary and St Philip was built by John Coventry, Lord of Burgate Manor, as a Servite monastery in 1873. It was transformed in 1984.

The Parish Church of St Mary's was rebuilt in 1150. Today it's mostly 13th to 15th century work, and it's full of activity. Pram Service 2nd Thursday. Family Service 3rd Sunday. Sign up for skittles or Marwell Zoo.

Historians disagree about its external wall tomb, but all admire the fine memorials, reredos, chests and mediaeval font . . . to say nothing of the choir under William Shering. Because you enter its airy glass-fronted porch (unusually) from the North, some say Saxon Fordingbridge may have lain to the South.

Two benefactors are remembered there — Catherine Eycott Bulkeley bought stock in 1801 to help pay for a Sunday School, (still going strong). John Dodington in 1638 arranged for £5 a year to be paid from Sandy Balls towards the apprenticing of poor children.

Above: Fordingbridge from the air in 1971.

Right: A great Fordingbridge occasion — the opening of the bypass in 1975.

Fordingbridge artist Stephen Martin (left) and Dennis Bailey, chairman of the Chamber of Trade, with the "Welcome to Fordingbridge" sign designed by Mr Martin, in 1978. It is featured on all the approach roads to the town.

Fordingbridge still looks after its young. In Penny's Lane is Mrs Rose Crouch's Infant School and the Junior School under Morris Patience. The well-equipped 500-pupil Burgate Comprehensive on the Salisbury Road opened as a Secondary School in 1957. At Sandle Manor, in a fine 1900 building built by the Hulses of Breamore, is a private preparatory school with 200 pupils. The porch is Elizabethan.

"Today, there are no bad children in Fordingbridge," says John Shering. "Just some not as good as others.'

FUTURE generations in Fordingbridge will be glad John Shering's 12-year-old daughter didn't know what a "gin trap" was.

"That's why I started the Museum," he says, "to show the young ones the old country things."

So now, 23 years later, you make your way through Shering's builder's yard and find yourself in a unique repository of Fordingbridge history.

The chronology and details may need to be sorted

out later. But in the Museum you'll savour Fordingbridge's most celebrated export — Neave's Farinaceous Food — through the 1898 Illustrated London News advertising its "flesh and bone-forming constitutents — as used by the Russian and Spanish Royal families".

At John Loader's, where today they sell animal feeds and generations of Bailey's have worked, old-timers will show you the "Cathedral" where Neaves had their corn mill, the site of Jack Hood's coal yard, the railway track ("ran right through this office, it did") and the sheds where the Tsar's baby food was packed.

Pete Lane remembers the 4.30 milk train. Leonard, his father, would get the train to stop "on the straight bit of track", so he could walk home. The obliging driver would toot the horn as he steamed past to warn mother he was coming.

The Railway hotel is now the Load of Hay . . . a name well-chosen for echoes of 1747. That was the year Smuggler King Captain Diamond escaped arrest, hiding his loot in a Whitsbury haywagon, while battle raged outside the George Inn.

John Shering's museum has old railway photographs and 1792 Fordingbridge-printed calico ("they've got some in the Vatican").

You can examine a bucketful of Fordingbridge teeth ("so much suffering there") extracted from a dentist's drain in the Greyhound Inn cellars.

I never pictured artist Augustus John playing cricket. But John will show you his subscription letter to the cricket club. Famous though he was, his colourful lifestyle and morals scandalised the townsfolk.

Visit hand-surgeon John Barron, who drank "gallons of sherry with him" if you want a fairer view. An "infinitely interesting patient", he was, says John, exotic. So were his friends and his bistro life. He spoke a number of Romany dialects and "would set off unexpectedly with his walking stick and 10-gallon hat to join the gipsies of Provence."

Top: Augustus John's studio at Fryern Court.
Below: Priscilla Thomas hand painting a porcelain vase at the Branksome China factory, housed in the old Regal cinema building in Shaftesbury Street.

The carpet of flowers in St Mary's church during the Domesday 900 celebrations in 1986.

The Albany Hotel started life as a temperance coffee house.

"If he liked you, he was relaxed and pleasant, but he could be diabolical," John Barron says. "His beard would stick out and his eyebrows go up and down.

" I remember going to see him once, lying painting on his bed, sheets covered with cigarette ash and sherry bottles all round."

"I'm much worse,' Augustus said. 'If you don't do my hand, I'll paint with my feet."

But John refused. "I knew his contractive disease

Right: The Rev. Roger Stirrup and St Mary's church.

JAMES COVENTRY BULKELEY
of Burgate Esqr.
died Nov. IV. MDCCLXIII.
Aged LVIII years.

Mrs. ANNE BULKELEY
of Burgate Spinster
died April XVII. MDCCLXXIII.
Aged LXXIV years.

Dame ANNE BULKELEY Relict of
Sr. DEWEY BULKELEY Kt. of Burgate.
Mother of the above JAMES and ANNE
BULKELEY, and Sister of the late Earl
COVENTRY, died Ap. XXIX: MDCCLXXIV
Aged CII Years.

The plaque to the Bulkeleys of Burgate Manor in the churchyard.

of the hand wouldn't respond to surgery. What's more if anything could go wrong with the operation, for Augustus it would. And he did paint (with his hands) to the end of his life."

Fordingbridge has had other controversial citizens. Rev. John Hall buried his first wife on May 5 1670 and conducted a wedding that day. He married his second wife on September 26 1670 and five months later, on February 10, baptized their child and conducted the burial service for his wife. He married his third wife in 1697 and died himself in 1700. Exhausted?

I left Shering's Museum with a jingle running through my mind:

Tis said of people in this Place
They are a very funny race
And one of their peculiar ways
They only get up alternate days.

Which John assured me was written up over the boathouse in the days when Fordingbridge was the Hampshire Henley.

FORDINGBRIDGE begins with the river. That much is clear - though much else still needs to be explored and local historians disagree among themselves.

There was certainly a prehistoric river crossing at Forde. The Saxons built two bridges. Was the town named for the fine seven-arched "Great Bridge" over the Avon? Then why was the church and ancient town centre so far away?

The "Lesser" or Leache Bridge over Sweatford and Allenwater Streams is tiny, but closer to the mediaeval village core round Church Square.

To confuse us all further, the present-day sprawl of Fordingbridge embraces three mediaeval manors — each with its own records, customs and bailiffs.

BORGATE was the oldest. It controlled the hundred from early times and built the 17th century Court House at the top of Green Lane. Bulkeleys were Lords of Burgate from the mid-15th century and Coventrys till the mid-20th.

By the late 1100s, WOODFIDLEY, the Rectory Manor, had been formed. At first Fordingbridge had a resident rector. He would have run the estates from Parsonage House. Then early in the 1400s, a Cambridge College became rector. To this day the Provost and scholars of King's College, as patrons, keep the chancel of St Mary's wind and weatherproof.

The third was FORDINGBRIDGE manor. For 680 years the Lord was the absentee Le Brune family (later Prideaux Brune). They preferred Padstow to the house at North Midgham. Their manorial records were intact until quite recently someone collected the great chest from their St Austell solicitor's. No-one can find them.

At least we have Domesday book. In 1086 the village in church square had two watermills and a church (value 30 shillings). There early market stalls were erected. Permanent shops followed. There were 100 acres of open-field arable, and two days' work due to the Lord at Harvest.

This was a poor market town, despite its two bridges. Few had to pay tax. Rockbourne and the surrounding villages (bar only Midgham and Bickton) were far more prosperous. Breamore Priory in 1348 had to promise to supply 3 shillings-worth of bread annually to 144 Fordingbridge paupers.

By the 13th century the market had moved to today's Royal Arms crossroads and with it the commercial heart. Church Square became residential.

Meantime, Fordingbridge was milling, and dyeing cloth. Four watermills stood here in the Middle Ages. Adam le Deyere was dyeing cloth near the Great Bridge in 1336. By the 18th century, everyone knew Fordingbridge for its high-quality serge, bed ticking, tanning, rope making and sailcloth for Buckler's Hard.

The shops in the present High Street are mostly 17th century or later.

Three terrible summer fires swept Fordingbridge in 40 years. On Wednesday, July 2 1662 15 houses were destroyed. Most devastating was the one on

Below: Fordingbridge Railway Station, circa 1930.

Below: The Market Square, circa 1905, with gas lamp.

Sunday June 23, 1672 when 102 households were burnt out. Damage to houses was £6751, to goods £6882. In 1702, there was £5059 19s 0d fire damage and collections were raised all over England.

By 1795 Sarah Rogers was heading the housewives' revolt against high prices. She got three months in jail.

Fordingbridge was then a "small but pleasant inland town", busy printing calico with 500 looms making ticking. Brookman's London waggon came every Monday afternoon at 4 and left on Tuesdays at 2. (Parcels to London 4 shillings). You could get to Salisbury by William Witcher's stage waggon from Poole (Weds) or William Watkins' cart from Ringwood (Tues and Sat, 8am).

This was a fruitful valley, says the Universal British Directory, with innumerable beautiful and rich water meadows, the surrounding hills on each side lined with remarkable fine timber and intercepted with gentlemen's seats . . .

It says nothing of the old cottages with "hidey holes" and convenient windows facing the forest for deer poaching. Queen Victoria's coronation was still to come. They roasted four sheep and an ox.

The Literary, Scientific and Mechanics Institute would be founded in 1850, gold would be found and Molly Parker would one day play the piano for the silent pictures. By 1923, Fordingbridge would even have 19 telephones.

Back in 1792, with the traffic jam yet to be invented and the Quakers a power in the area, the Avon was highly prized.

"This river which from different small streams unites at Salisbury, runs from thence through Downton, Fordingbridge and Ringwood and empties itself into the sea at Christchurch, adds very much to the fruitfulness of the Vale."

This was before there were 22 trout farms north of Downton and farmers used artifical fertilizers. Which is why the townsfolk are banding together to protect their river.

The Salisbury coach in Bridge Street, circa 1900.

The Great Bridge at Fordingbridge on a sunny day in May 1956.

Fovant

On the first Sunday in July the little village of Fovant (electoral roll 576) draws old soldiers and sightseers from all over the world to the annual Drumhead service.

That crowd includes men who rose at 4 am to cut huge army regimental badges into the 800-foot-high chalk downland, in 1916.

"At 7 am, when the firing ranges opened, we would slide down on our shovels," the old soldiers say.

The famous badges — twelve in all — include a map of Australia. Sentimentalists say the 1916 soldiers facing the prospect of the trenches in France, "wanted to leave something of themselves behind." Cynics see them as military graffiti.

But much effort goes into maintaining and restoring them. They have to be cut anew each year. Some have actually disappeared.

Visitors patronise the Pembroke Arms and Cross Keys pubs, visit the Australian War Graves and peer at the 1495 brass at St George's Church, a mile away.

They may well meet farmer David Harris exercising seven prize Blonde D'Aquitaine bulls in their unique walking frame.

They may meet Ron Braybrook, the butcher, playing the church organ or find themselves admiring honey-coloured Chilmark stone houses in the High Street.

But they will need to pry a little to find the deeper roots of Fovant.

An undrained tangled swamp in prehistoric times . . . Neolithic, Bronze Age, Iron Age settlers on the ridges . . . and then in 552 AD Saxons from Jutland founded Fobbanfunta at the foot of the downs.

King Alfred knew Fovant, Aethelred gave it to the rich Wilton convent, and in 1539 when Henry the Eighth took it back, where did he exile the abbess and nuns to? Fovant, of course. They are remembered in the old name — Nun's Walk — for Nightingale Lane (which leads unromantically to the sewage works).

There are other names which bring back the past. "Koppergon" is where the bobby lived. "Touching Head Copse" is near today's First School. Unlike Fovant's 1782 establishment it does not offer "an exceedingly good cold bath."

The A30 turnpike opened in 1761 (4½d per carriage and 1½d per rider). 1784 saw the first Royal Mail coach, with horses changed every 11 miles. The Pembroke Arms stables jingled.

There were highwaymen and smugglers, poachers caught in Fovant Wood, Guilds, Pig clubs, Brass and Silver bands. But quiet Fovant really awoke with the building of vast army camps in 1914.

Mrs Edna Coombes, whose wedding cakes are legendary, has known Fovant for over 70 years. Officers were billeted on her parents ("I can still see myself aged three in one of the army huts in my red velvet dress, sitting on an officer's knee.")

That was when the branch railway was being built from Dinton, the military hospital and the "Picture Palace" of which only the steps remain.

What's more, the famous medical Clay family were already in residence at The Manor House.

Above: The famous Garrison cinema at Fovant. The steps with their urns outlasted the "Picture Palace" and have been copied for the new bungalow recently built there.

Roy Nuttall, Parish Council chairman, posts a letter in the Victorian postbox.

Right: A view from Fovant Hollow, from which one of the finest downland vistas in Wiltshire can be seen.

Mrs Edna Coombes, whose life has revolved around Fovant village activities, outside the village hall she cared for during the war.

Below: A bird's eye view of the famous Fovant Badges, showing Chislebury Camp, the circular earthwork, above.

"Old Doctor Clay" is the hero of many a tale of early Fovant — how he "sat beside me with mumps until I ate a boiled egg," how "he tried out his first stitches on my mother-in-law," how he "was everybody's friend."

He, it was, who wrote the first popular history of Fovant (since then updated and illustrated by Roy Nuttall, Parish Council Chairman).

Today Fovant still has its own doctor, his surgery in a converted stable block near the Victorian letter box.

It has a fish farm (50-60 tons of rainbow trout a year) where the watercress beds once flourished.

Fovant has an antique furniture restorer, Brian Walker. He has helped to do up the magnificent 1880 fairground Rodeo switchback housed at Stainers Garage.

There's a Chapel and, behind the Poplars pub, a forgotten Quaker burial ground; near the other pubs stand the Stocks.

Fovant breaks many rules. The old people's bungalows aren't near the shops. The bus shelter is off the bus route. The church is out of sight of the village.

But it still has a thriving village life; gravediggers like Charlie Foyle and Hedley Jarvis, natural entertainers like Bill Foyle who will don a smock and sing, villagers who remember banging tin trays ("Give us a song, Jessie") in the pubs . . . as well as cricket club, football club, WI, Youth Club and a Poors Charity to help with fuel bills.

There are of course the "weekenders" from London, and the predatory backland developers.

But the overall verdict is a good one. . . "I wouldn't live anywhere else.". . . "It was a newcomer — an RAF wife — who laid on the pensioners' entertainment this year." . . . "I'd say there were still three levels of communication — TELEPHONE, TELEGRAPH and TELL THE BUTCHER.". . . "We always spot a stray dog. But we don't any longer know all the faces."

Godshill

BEFORE 1950, before tarmac roads, electricity and water, the forest fringe smallholders of Godshill ate a hearty breakfast and were self-reliant, hard-working and thrifty.

"We were a master race," says Charlie White, chuckling.

You kept potatoes in an earth clamp, neighbour helped neighbour ("that's how you survived"), everyone ran animals and hunted in the forest ("Mind you, you could recognise the gentry") and every week you walked your animals to Ringwood market and Salisbury.

Godshill was full of Chalks and Whites, Witts, Groves, Sturgesses and Cutlers when Mrs Mellors ("the lion tamer") arrived as schoolmistress in 1922. Millionaire Oliver Cutts had not arrived, nor Barbara Castle's parents.

Children like Ada Witt played in the road. There was an annual Breamore House tea and a Sunday School treat to Bournemouth by waggonette and train.

There's still some home-brewed cider about in Godshill. But the erstwhile working village is now expensive and leisure-minded with riding lessons and pottery, the Godshill Players and WI and the Sandy Balls village-within-a-village (2,500 campers a week in season). Their indoor pool is the in-thing.

Lady Hulse's (1903) Village Hall is well used and St Giles' Church seats 60. The post office shop survives. But the Chapel and school have closed, like the Quaker meeting.

Charlie White collected the thatch of the old "Fighting Cocks" as pig litter in 1929 when the Southampton Road was widened. That's when today's smart pub replaced the smugglers den.

Retired publicans Jim and Barbara Grigg have a pair of cockspurs unused since 1849. You can still see the cock pit outline on the grass.

It's near the Great Pond where experts study Godshill's unique "Fairy Shrimp"... a primitive inch-long crustacean, Cheirocephalus diaphanus, which has 11 pairs of leaf-like limbs and lives only in temporary pools.

Some say it was the war that made Godshill famous. Certainly, here they tested the first prototype of Barnes Wallis' Dambusters bouncing bomb.

But Godshill is on a ley line and near the Avon river-thoroughfare. Neolithic scrapers show that early man found shelter here on a bleak 200-foot gravel escarpment north-east of Fordingbridge. Prehistoric Godman's Cap camp (10,000-3,000 BC) still awaits excavation.

Above: Jim and Barbara Grigg, retired publicans, pictured wth a memento from the old signpost which stood outside this famous pub.

Left: Jean Cormack with some of her organically grown produce from Sandy Balls.

Ada Witt with an oil painting of the village she knew in her youth.

Photocall for the Godshill Sunday School before their outing in 1914.

In Roman times it was a centre for wheel-turned pottery. Today all that's left of a major trading highway is a bridle path known as "Potters Way".

Ambrosius and Arthur camped here in AD 514 and gave it its name. It was "Hulle or Hullum" in 1217 and "Godeshull" in 1403. The 1217 "Geel's Spring" has become Giles Well ("which old Mr Cutler used")."Arniss Farm" is an old name, too (1217: Arneys, 1801: Erne's House).

From 1410, under 12 monarchs the Ringwoods owned "Goddeshill Manor with Foldes and Sandyballes". From 1392, "Cridlestowe alias East Mylle" held the Manor court, in a house behind Shepherd's Spring restaurant.

In 1592, Squire William Dodington of Breamore House bought Godshill. He was the forerunner of the Hulses who owned Godshill until 1919 when "the young captain was killed".

Over the centuries, the Commoners Rights and Duties in the Forest are documented and fiercely defended. After all, their ancestors had lost everything when William created the forest.

In 1583 they claimed the forest timber and turf, the right to run hogs, cattle and horses and the first drift of colts and hogs. In exchange they kept the forest fenced, maintained three drifts and the pound.

Once, it was said, "Sandy Balles" was the home of witches and goblins. From 1919 Ernest Westlake's ideas on "learning by doing" also mystified indigenous Godshillers. But now the home of his birth in Fordingbridge is to have a commemorative blue plaque.

He set up the Grithfyrd at Sandy Balls as a communal experiment for the unemployed. (The name means Positive Peace Army in Anglo-Saxon.)

Then there was his 1916 pacifist cradle-to-grave Order of Woodcraft Chivalry. Children at his 1928 Forest School swam naked, danced, and ran about barelegged. There was talk of arson and an unexplained 1928 fire.

Today, for other reasons, the village is unsure about Sandy Balls. ("Such crowds!") There lives Jean Cormack (historian, biodynamic market gardener and artist), Councillor Martin Westlake and Richard, MD of the holiday centre "ranked the best in the south".

Among the tall pines (near the Dowser Society walnut tree) is the Westlake family burial ground, including the grave of longserving councillor Aubrey, a doctor "ahead of his time".

They roll eggs down Good Friday Hill, they treasure "Aunt Eliza's" watercolours and their restored gypsy caravan. But times have changed since Ada Witt "collected wortleberries, when there was only a keeper's cottage there."

Today thousands pass through and some 120, like the Morrises, stay. They showed me their spectacular view, garden and retirement home.

"This is our little bit of heaven," they said.

Right: Harvest time at Godshill in the 1900's

Great Wishford

ALEC Moulding, with his stick, his long memory, and his passion for the history of building materials, is the perfect companion for a visit to Great Wishford.

He has a personal link with every brick, flint, cob wall and cottage. He helped get the 1728 Richard Newsham fire engine into the church in 1972 ("and it was a tight squeeze I can tell you"). He knew those who saw the stocks in use, and (a longtime secret) he carved three of the famous breadstones on the churchyard wall.

Richard Moulding, his father, built the last cob house "in the old-fashioned way" in England, for the gardener of Druid's Lodge in the days of racing millionaire A.F. Cunlithe. He has photographs to prove no plywood or shuttering was used.

To Alec, the characters in the tiny village's history are as familiar as old friends. Their names are as well known to him as the famous cries of "Grovely, Grovely, Grovely and All Grovely" and the banging of tin cans which arouse every household before dawn on Oak Apple Day, May 29.

There are not many "big names" associated with Great Wishford today. Lord Pembroke, of Wilton House still owns Manor Farm, where the Huntleys live, and Wishford Farm, (once the home of Sir Edward Knatchbull) where the Thatchers live. More significantly, Lord Pembroke owns Grovely Wood, famous for its "hankshent custom" . . . "on girt Oak Apple Day."

Colonel Christopher Ross, ex-army and now Diocesan Secretary, lives at Wishford House behind its flagpole and fine early 18th century brick facade.

The widow of Lieutenant-Colonel H. Jones, VC, the Falklands hero, lives in a fine house ("and she's a nice lady and has mucked in well with the village.").

Lady Paskin, widow of Sir John, Under-Secretary of State in the Colonial Office, lives in a chequered cottage near the pub. She founded the regional history magazine, The Hatcher Review. The scholarly booklet on Wishford's St Giles Church is also hers

Left: The Oak Apple Day celebrations are featured on the sign of the Royal Oak.

Below: St Giles and the village centre.

George Hayward, the chairman of Wishford Oak Apple Club, with his staff of office. He is responsible for the annual celebrations on May 29, Oak Apple Day.

Below: Percy and Violet Dewey, who have lived more than 48 years in their South Street cottage with their personal oak tree, which is decorated each Oak Apple Day.

(with an introduction by Sir John Betjeman).

Since the 1890s the Wilton Flyfishing Club headquarters have been in Wishford. The riverkeeper has always lived in the village too, Lady Paskin says.

But craftman-historian Alec Moulding is concerned to introduce you to Nicholas (d 1386) and Edith de Bonham in the church, now recovered from the shock of producing septuplets after a seven year separation. Sir Richard Grobham lies in magnificent repose in his 1629 marbled monument beside his (slightly lower and quickly remarried) widow.

Thirty-three cherubs look down from the coffered arch in the chancel, and two angels weep nearby. Steward to Sir Thomas Gorges, he profited well from the treasure aboard a Spanish galleon wrecked near Hurst Castle.

His are the dormered almshouses opposite the church with their layers of identical-sized flints. ("He must have searched the whole valley to find those matching flints," says Alec Moulding.) He can show you 11 cottages showing Grobham's hallmark.

Sir Richard Howe endowed the school in 1722 for 20 poor boys and 20 poor girls "to write, read, cast accounts and learn and say the church catechism." His craftsmen produced wonderful brickwork in Flemish bond, painstakingly using blue kiln end bricks to create the patterns.

Charles II chose Oak Apple Day in 1660 to make Sir Richard's father, John, a baronet. That is the day Great Wishford villagers reaffirm their ancient firewood rights in Grovely Wood.

Even today the festivities begin at 3am. Oak branches cut in the wood festoon the houses and churchtower, costumed 19th century women dance on Salisbury's Cathedral Green, and the 1603 charter is read before the altar. Later the village echoes to bands, dancing and carnival.

The Oak Apple Club (chairman, George Hayward, president, the rector) is limited to the 328 who live here. The exclusive club began at the end of a legal battle in 1895 to preserve the villagers' ancient rights.

Great Wishford boasts exquisite cob houses, cruck cottages, and chequer-patterned walls. There is a fine palladian house, now altered, and thatched walls along the main street.

But Wishford also boasts an early example of retail price statistics on its churchyard wall. Eight carved stones record the price of bread "per gallon" (that's four 2lb loaves) since 1800.

"You see this valley, from early times, was famous for bread through sheep," says Alec Moulding, pausing to let it sink in.

"They were reared in this valley on all the hills, to provide fertiliser for the corn which made bread as well as the wool and the meat."

There's no village for miles around with such history, in its very stones, he says. And he's right.

Right: Builder Alec Moulding with the famous bread stones — a permanent reminder of the rising cost of living since 1800. Alec carved the three most recent ones.

Hindon

HINDON today (Population 488) is smart and compact with its tree-lined High Street, wide pavements, and well-kept Chilmark stone houses.

"Things are so altered," the old ones say. "Hindon was a poor village in the days when you woke to the sound of labourers' hobnail boots tramping up the High Street, when our mothers took in washing, put new feet in old stockings and everyone drew water for the copper after church on a Sunday night."

There are still a handful who "wouldn't feel right" in church without a hat, who remember curtseying to the doctor's wife and Lady Octavia (Shaw-Stewart) in her long black gown and cloak.

They speak of bread and calico at Christmas, dropping candle grease on the doorstep when they went round carol singing, "sitting out" to do the peas and beans . . . and front doors that were never closed.

Mrs May Gray has the oldest memories. Born in 1897, they called her Jubilee as a child. She has lived in Hindon for over 90 years.

It's hard to picture a Hindon in which tired working men spent every evening in the Reading Room at the foot of the High Street. ("Mr Hugh Morrison gave it to us.")

Today many retired people choose Hindon and there are few children. By contrast, its 1868 school roll was 125. (Children sent home for "uncleanness in the person". Truancy for gleaning, acorn and potato-picking.) Today's Mrs Jan May's 42 pupils come from four villages.

"Textures" in the Old Bakery advertises basic astrology, organic produce and the osteopath; there's an antique shop, a delicatessen, (game in season, knitting wool), a post office shop, Butler garage and a bus shelter.

The "town of 14 pubs" is left with two. The Lamb (where Mrs Griffin was born) and the Grosvenor's Arms nod at each other at the crossroads.

The Methodist Chapel has closed. Basil Bevis, retired stonemason, keeps the key. Inside you'll find golden flowerheads, looms and spinning wheels and expensive handmade textiles.

For 652 years Hindon folk had to hike to East Knoyle to be married. Strange, because this was (like Downton) a New Town carefully-planned by Bishop des Roches. But he only gave it a Chapel of Ease.

In 1970 the church was 100 years old. Hindon is full of historians, and they celebrated the centenary with a Victorian Street Market.

The present authority on this "pre-industrial town devastated by fire and rebuilt in 1754, this notorious rotten borough, market and posting town" is former translator, Norah Shears.

She's unearthed not only Hindon's story (£2), but its photographs and the 1748 Calthorpe map in the Village Hall.

Hindon began in 1219. Home to "thieves, poachers and ruffians", it became a stupefyingly rotten borough. William of Orange visited it. It had its Swing riots in 1830. John Beckett, would-be rioter, was locked in the belfry for safe-keeping by his wife.

"We still have the burgesses' strip gardens," says Miss Shears. "And here's where the fire started."

Then there are the Shell and the Dolphin stones from Beckford's Fonthill Abbey, the pierced archways for coaches and the 1775 town crier's bell.

In 1922 the Hindon estate was sold and for many a self-sufficient homogeneous world came to an end. ("That were the worst day's work ever.")

Till then most people worked for the Morrisons. Water came from wells. The carrier went to Salisbury on Tuesdays and Saturdays. They had three bakers,

Basil Bevis, retired stonemason, outside the former Methodist Chapel, now used as a craft centre.

Below: Hindon Band in the late 1930s.

Below: The ruins of the war memorial after a tank demolished it during the last war. It was rebuilt at a cost of £440, of which £406 was War Office compensation.

two grocers, post office and a butcher.

Large families depended on home-grown produce and everything shown at the Flower Show was grown in manure from the family pig.

They collected birds' nests, hazel nuts and chestnuts in the Abbey Woods, mushrooms on the unploughed downland and armfuls of primroses on Good Friday. Lady Octavia gave holly at Christmas and the school treat. ("We took our own cups and you could eat as much as you liked.")

Money was short. "You can have my son to help you out" was a way of repaying debts. Loose ears of corn went to chickens. Mrs Stevens, who laid out the dead, left children "a nest of apples" by her back gate.

Henry Doughty had a sawbench and tackle and thrashing machine. "But that steam engine plough and tackle used to plough too deep." It was a blacksmith, Brian Coombes, who bought Hindon's first car.

Hindon, once so stable, has changed. An American tank demolished the War Memorial. The licensed Fellowship Club killed off the Reading Room. The gipsies have gone from the Dene.

There's a Good Companions Club, a voluntary car service, a WI and British Legion. There's also warmth below the apparent sophistication.

For I left beautiful Hindon tucked into its rolling downland, not merely humbled by its history, but warmed by cups of tea and carrying a bunch of homegrown flowers and a knitting pattern.

Above: "I've only spent six weeks away from Hindon in 90 years." said Mrs May Gray, Hindon's oldest born-and-bred resident.

Right: The Lamb Inn is one of two surviving public houses. In its heyday, Hindon had 14.

Below: Out for the day! A Reading Room charabanc outing in 1929.

Idmiston, Porton & Gomeldon

IDMISTON, Porton and Gomeldon — east and west — are brimming with newcomers. Few of them have time to speculate on the unknown Saxon Idma, who gave his name to their parish, to wonder about Perortone or why Gumba's Dun, a mile up the road, came into their patch.

Most of its 2,250 people live in new houses and more than half work at the neighbouring military and RAF camps. They are mobile and energetic. Few show any interest in peace camps, animal rights protesters or women who stop trains and cut fences.

There are many ways to learn of Idmiston's past. Try Alderbury Hundred Rolls, "Ex antiquo", they say, Glastonbury Abbey has owned "Eumestetone". In the ancient charters of Glastonbury church is one giving "faithful" Wulfic five Idmistone farms (signed King Eddred, AD 948), Aelfswyth the Nun (perhaps doubly faithful?) got ten farms from King Edgar in AD 970. And then of course, comes the Domesday book.

A much easier route is through David Ride's little 1983 booklet. It begins with the formation of rocks and fossils and ends with the Chemical Defence Establishment, birds and animal life.

He ought to be an authority. His archaeological apprenticeship was served in the dust of Porton Down, digging, sifting and recording. There are over 200 monuments, barrows and ditches up there on "the MOD's star conservation site."

David and his wife can tell of the exhilaration and the slog of five summer holidays spent exploring a Bronze Age burial site (seven pot cremations in a line). Stonehenge was the religous headquarters of a much larger cultural complex.

David will tell you how they found flints which had been part of three different cultures — first, Neolithic man who dug flint mines at Porton 5,000 years ago; then the bank and ditch builders of 500 BC who reused the waste from the ancient mines. Finally, 250 years ago, gunflint knappers quarried there. The flints they found were used to fire 18th century muskets.

Doing your homework can be of practical use, too. The famous tractor driver, who fell into one of three underground tunnels leading to Idmiston church, had obviously not done his reading.

One tunnel led from the 1628 Old Rectory, until 1828 the home of the Bowle family. "Don" Bowle, a 1750 vicar called John, first translated Don Quixote into English. The latest Bowle was buried in Idmiston in 1985.

At Idmiston Manor (another tunnel) lived General Monck who helped Charles II back to power, despite his earlier support for Cromwell.

And there was scandal, as well as a tunnel, at the Old Vicarage (where legend claims Charles I once hid). There in 1589, Curate Edmund Rideout "had his pleasure" with his housekeeper Joane Payne "until she was with child", then exiled her to West Dean. What the bishop said is not recorded.

The old postman, Charlie Tompkins, has written down his memories of agricultural Idmiston, which lasted until the 1930s ... a community where Salisbury was "New Sarum", harvests affected everyone, and everyone's dread was "parish relief".

Above: A lone cyclist makes his way up Porton High Street in 1946.

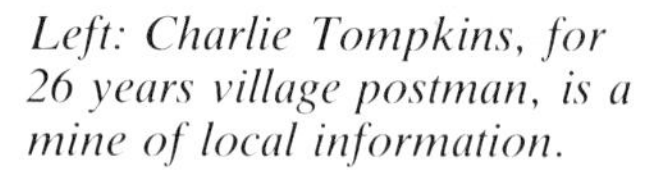

Left: Charlie Tompkins, for 26 years village postman, is a mine of local information.

Edwardian children outside Bell Cottage, when it was a school and pupils paid three pennies a week for their schooling.

Above: Wheeltappers on the track at Porton railway station in the early 1900s.

Below: The Porton Hotel, the only village public house, once stood beside the station.

Above: The upper class of Idmiston School in 1932.

Then Porton railway station served farmers from as far as Woodford and Durnford. Farm waggon wheels rattled by, harness bells jingled, and milk was sent to Wimbledon twice a day.

The Bourne Valley Flower show was on Birdlymes Farm and Black Minorca's "always took first for white eggs." No one today could dig a well as straight as Mr Hobbs of Gomeldon and Old Jimmy Crouch. A spoon would stand up in Fred White's dairy shorthorns' milk and Christmas and Good Friday were the only paid holidays.

Till 1913, sewage was dug with a spudgel, mixed with ashes, and dried. ("Hard work, not pleasant"). The effluent produced lots of tomato plants.

Derrick and Dorothy Bailey were born and bred here in "an interlocking family community". He went to bed with a candle and drew water from a well. Mothers helped with others' mending. Pig food potatoes were coloured mauve, and smelt dreadful as they boiled in the copper.

The fathers checked their watches by the railway clock. Hunchback Mr Buckle, with his long beard, would cycle from Salisbury with cotton, elastic and shoelaces and Mr Dodd sold knitting wool from his Austin 7.

Boys went beating for the toffs, fished, found wild ducks eggs and sold pheasant nests for 6d. There was primrosing in Bentley Wood.

But the story I most enjoyed of Old Porton town, was not of bike rides to Frome or walks to Salisbury, wartime concerts at the camps or friendly Australian troops . . . it was of little Derrick Bailey's Sunday afternoons talking stamps at "Rose Moor" with Fred Bates.

Unknown to anyone he was a German spy who sent signals from the willow trees by the river. Derrick heard him ask his wife, "Is the teapot hot?" Until 1946 when "Fritz Battes" was caught in Bristol, no-one guessed that "teapot" was an aerial.

THE PARISH of Idmiston is unusual, says the 1975 parish council handout. To start with, it includes three villages — quiet Idmiston, burgeoning Porton, and Gomeldon, apart.

But that's not all.

It must be one of the best fortified parishes since the days of the walled city. There's Porton Down and Boscombe Down close by, complete with perimeter fences. Red notices prohibit CB radios and cameras, promote the Official Secrets Act and shout Danger Danger Danger. You are within earshot of Bulford and Larkhill *("They bang away all night but you get used to it").*

A Wellington bomber landed in a Porton conker tree which now has an extraordinary shape.

A copse is named after Moll Harris the Highwaywoman (but no-one knows much about her shape). Salisbury Museum looks after a 3000-year-old dog they found there and the Royal College of Surgeons a 700 year old skeleton with all its teeth. Everywhere there's history and controversies ancient and modern. But few realise the abundance of wildlife — Look for badgers, butterflies and junipers on the 7,000 acres of land behind the wire; kingfishers, swans, foxes and herons in the watermeadows and trout in the river. Ask the children at the Wednesday Watch Club, and they'll show you the orchids and cowslips, too.

"It's a well-organised, convenient, nice place to live. Nice people live here," one resident said to me. The trains have stopped. But there are buses, and the laundry, wet fish, greengrocery and fish and chips come to your door.

"We benefit from our mobile population," says David Ride. "They get on and integrate from day one."

In Porton there's plenty to do, from swings and slides to a flower club, old time dancing, drama,

Scouts, choir and a Sunshine Club. Mr Conduit, the butcher, stocks game, and you'll find a newsagent, post office, wine shop, hairdresser and a garage. Gomeldon lacks a hall, but has a versatile school and a grocer.

Landscape gardeners have set up in the old railway station. Nearby, Porton Hotel is going strong, with a picture of its 1921 fire in the hall.

They've done badly on pubs since April, 1775. *"I am entirely averse to the having of any Alehouse within the Parish of Idmiston, Porton, Gumbleton and cannot but think such a house must be productive of bad consequences to the said parish,"* said John Bowle when Anthony Cole was caught selling booze from home.

Charlie Tompkins tells of an off-licence brew house at the old thatched Post Office ("They sat on the bank opposite and drank the beer."). The thirsty must now seek "bad consequences" outside the parish at the Plough on the A338 or the Pheasant on the A30.

It is the Memorial Hall which draws this extraordinary parish together, says Charles Pude, long-time district councillor. So does concern for a footpath from Idmiston to the school, the hope of a branch surgery — there's no doctor — and the traffic on the A338 "county distributor route."

When you walk along the lane past the medieval village in the "Humpy Field", you see on the skyline the windmill, brought here by night, which ground barley till 1885. Below you, where the Roman Portway to Silchester fords the Bourne, there are oaks and willows and the herringbone pattern of the watermeadow channels.

The Reverend Sykes has newly arrived in the parish. Idmiston's beautiful All Saints' Church is now "redundant", replaced by Porton's 19th century St Nicholas. The Methodist Chapel is now a house, the Lifeboat Chapel has disappeared, but the 1865 Baptist Chapel in Porton High Street is alive and well. They began earlier in secret at Birdlymes Farm but Porton Baptists met openly in Porton in 1655. Among their flock was Civil War JP John Rede, who was hanged at Devizes. His grave — vandalised — is in the little council-kept Winterslow Road cemetery.

There are, of course, two schools. Idmiston School is in Porton and covers Boscombe and Allington, too. Here in an open-plan modern school overlooking the river, Mrs Jan Jones has 114 children.

It's a far cry from the old days, when Derek Bailey says: "It was a mountaineering expedition to play football. We often had to stand in the corner with our hands on our heads and write out our spellings 100 times after school. I remember only one 'away' match."

Gomeldon Primary School (opened 1912 for the children of the smallholders) was the brainchild of Rev Youngman. Records tell of days off for potato picking and to see the Wild Beast Show. Today, it is a happy little school with about 90 pupils, says head teacher, Miss Helen Scott.

But there's been a "tragedy." Gales have snapped its famous flagpole in two.

"Old pupils think we have closed," Miss Scott says. "We've always flown the flag."

Above: Rooftops of Idmiston . . . a rural view of the village from the hill behind All Saints Church.

Below: Former rector, Rev. John Harvey, during a sponsored read-in on a chilly January day in 1985 at St Nicholas' church, Porton. To keep out the cold, Mr Harvey took with him a few wee drams of whisky and water.

The children of Gomeldon Primary School in 1987.

Landford

BEFORE the First World War, Landford was only agriculture and big houses and church and chapel didn't mix. That Landford has completely disappeared. The girls of all classes wear silk stockings . . .

Midway between Salisbury and Southampton, Landford (1981 pop: 1163) is a modern, if scattered village. Motorists whizzing along the A36 see only restaurants, garden centre, Crusader carpets ("where the best costs less") and secondhand cars, videos and petrol.

For this village-without-a-pub straddles the old turnpike "tarmacked in a hurry in the bad winter of 1916 when the frost got into the chalk and spewed up the gravel. I remember army lorries cluttered up right over Pepperbox."

Otho's Domesday village (worth 15 shillings with 2 hides, 2 ploughlands, 6 borderers and a Mill paying 20 pence) centred around the church. No-one has claimed King Alfred's 9th century Leonaford house, but they are proud of their prehistoric Cloven Way, Iron Age Burial Mound and 5000-year-old Stone Age remains.

The modern village to the west of the A36 grew up in Victorian times on the rough grazing land between the 1842 school and Dibden's celebrated bakery (lardy and dough cakes a speciality). There's no village hall but a Post Office and shop, the yellow brick Methodist Chapel, the red brick Beech Grange estate, a fruit farm and recreation ground down a rough track. And long village memories.

Retired shoemaker Reg King was expected to die as a child. Great-grandson of one of the founding Primitive Methodists and one of seven, he sang under Miss Olive and Sir Adrian Boult with the Landford Choral Society and enjoyed the wildlife of his farm childhood. In 1921, when the well dried up, they carried water half a mile.

Above: A pair of Kings . . . Retired shoemaker Reg King (left) has known Landford for more than 80 years while Bill King (no relation) only moved there in 1910!

Below: Landford Manor as a stately home in 1915. Today it's a map-making centre.

Above: Local historian Stephen Ings by the grave of Mary Stanley, Queen of the Gypsies.

Bill King has completed 70 years in the church choir. He remembers how in 1913 he earned his half-sovereign from General Sir George Luck ("gruff with a heart of gold") for pumping the church organ. It bought him a suit for 9s.11d.

"It was a miracle how our folks managed" — coarse oatmeal and beef dripping from the big houses. Three-pennorth of bones boiled with vegetables was delicious sliced cold.

Sidney Penny has been baker, shopkeeper and part-time postman. He left school to learn icing and decorating from Mr Beckley in New Road whose sugar flowers and medallions were famous.

In 1931 a lad of 14 worked all hours for 10/- a week. One dark night, cycling up Glebe Lane on his blue Stop-me-and-buy-One Alldays and Onions delivery tricycle, Sidney's lamp ran out of carbide. "The copper fined me 5 shillings, checked why I was out so late (it was 9.30) and fixed me up with more carbide."

Sidney keeps the Methodist minute books and he treasures "Shops in the Village since 1900" — a school project by his son Graham, aged 12.
Before World War I, Graham tells us, "petrol was supplied in two-gallon sealed cans. These had to be stored in a locked pit built at the bottom of the garden." They saw the first petrol pumps outside Hatch's smithy at Earldoms tollgate.

"To buy food in a tin was almost a crime . . . Going to town was a very rare thing for any woman, so Mrs Henbest had a very good trade in calico."

Sorting and delivering the post was at first one of the duties of schoolmaster Newey (who also kept two owls in a cage at the school gate.) Later Latchmore Cottage was to be grocer, telephone exchange, post-office, bakery and cobbler.

Stephen Ings is only 36 but he knows his Landford. He showed me in the churchyard the stone to Mrs Mary Stanley, Queen of the Gipsies, whose 1797 funeral ("with great numbers of gipsies dressed in black velvet") was described by William Harrison's grandfather.

There is also the memorial to Robert Beck who "on Old Christmas Day 1793" fell out of an Oak Tree which he "erroneously" expected to burst into bud.

In the 1858 church, largely paid for (like the school) by Countess Nelson at the Manor, you'll find a churchyard cross and Norman doorway taken from its predecessor.

Eyres and Nelsons at the Manor House were to be succeeded by cotton millionaire Fred Pannizzi (nicknamed Bulldog) and known as Preston. Like Mrs Wigram of Northlands who insisted on curtseys in the street, they say the last private owner of the Manor reported pupils who didn't doff their caps. Today large-scale maps are printed in the Manor.

Landford Wood Mission Hall, a beautiful wooden chapel, is near Melchet Court, now a school. Sir Alfred Mond, who founded ICI, was to become the first Lord Melchet under Lloyd George. Reg King remembers taking him a telegram by bicycle.

Today there are wine grapes at Brooklands, where Alan Haikney of Optica lives, and there's a nursery on the cricket field to which a long-ago rector sent barrels of beer.

"This morning the stench of tobacco smoke and beer is almost unbearable" — (School log 1889)

Now Landford is full of commuters. Much new energy comes from Beech Grange, once viewed with misgivings. There's no school truancy at harvest and haymaking and no-one plays Kit-Kat (Poor Man's Cricket). "But we all rub along pretty well,"Sid Penny says.

The picturesque timbered Landford Wood Mission Hall.

Above: The Methodist Sunday School outing to Southsea in 1931 featuring Sidney Penny, aged 14 (centre of picture in cap).

Below: Landford schoolchildren about 1956.

The Langfords

STEEPLE, Hanging and Little Langford — they all got their surnames from the long ford across the Wylye, on the path used as a shortcut to Stonehenge.

Today Steeple Langford has the traffic, the shop, the school, two pubs and a resident rector.

Hanging Langford, its senior, has the village hall, more houses, a largely executive and mobile population, a red postbox set in the thatched Manor House wall and trains rushing by.

Little Langford, the oldest, is a tiny hamlet where a village vanished to make way for the railway.

There you must visit chequered St Nicholas' church, if only to see St Aldhelm's burgeoning staff, the boarhunt on the lintel, and a noseless one-legged Elizabethan in his ruff lying in the south chantry.

Then follow the old Saxon road from Wilton to Warminster up the peaceful valley. Under the (non-Saxon) railway bridge to Hanging Langford where the oldest born-and-bred resident, Mrs Mavis James, is only in her 50s.

Hanging Langford lost its station in the 1860s (though you can find it under a hedge behind White Cottage) so locals who had to disembark at Wylye used to throw their parcels out of the window when they reached Hanging Langford.

In the past 22 years, it has lost its chapel, its butcher, Conduit's bakery, its shop — and, in 1966, The Railway Tavern where for 52 years Mrs Annie Witt served Ushers beer from wooden barrels ("the best pint ever").

"The Darts Team down at the Railway/They reckon is second to none/Derrick James is their popular skipper/you should see all the prizes he's won," they wrote in Ushers "Mashtun". He's still got them, too.

Most of his working life was spent as a platelayer on the railway ("hard work but enjoyable"). He'll describe fettling the track, "jacking it up, shovel-packing it and slewing it back in proper alignment. He'll speak of bullheads, and chippings, chairs and bearings, and how "on a curve a rail can be as high as 5 inches".

"If you didn't wrap your hands in cotton waste, your hands could freeze to the iron bars," he said. One of his original gang of five, Cecil Thring, still lives nearby.

Above: Ploughing with a Fordson Standard tractor on the downs above Steeple Langford in the 1930s.

Right: Bill Henderson, author and local historian, shortly before his death in 1988.

"Hanging" like "henge" means something precipitous that sticks up, said Bill Henderson who died recently. Tucked under its hill along the Wylye Road, Hanging Langford today has a fast-changing population.

"Despite what people think," said Bill," it's the new ones who give most to today's community life" ... village hall quarterly dinners, evening classes, the fete, the fishing, the WI. ("But it's Mavis James and Mrs Dennis who run the Welcome Club.")

After 40 years Wain and Georgie Helyer feel "nearly local". Between lambs, Georgie edits the Messenger, a 560-copy free community magazine.

Down near the watermeadows and the bridge which connects the two larger Langfords, a new-born Temel ram lamb was shivering and struggling to his feet.

The birth of the lambs in the Langford valley is still one of the timeless dramas of Spring. Even after a pilgrimage to the Holy Land, Georgie was breathless.

"By breeding he might make a champion," she said.

There are still a few of the old born-and-bred villagers left who remember weeding the A303 ("Castle Road"), which led to long ago fairs at Yarnborough Castle.

One of the indomitable characters from the past was Grandmother Emma Thring, a hard taskmaster and tireless. "She never came back from Grovely Wood without a hitch of wood."

It was the valuable flints for the roads which led her to buy Hill View Farm. Grand-daughter Dorothy Crozier had to spend school holidays collecting them. ("We got 6d for a yard of stones measured by a string.")

They were piled in the laybys, reloaded on to carts, cracked and rollered in. Later came the horsedrawn tar barrel, with a man walking behind to spread it.

In those days, the cider press called in the autumn to crush your apples in the orchard, and they drew water for the trains from the well by the village hall.

It was enterprising Emma (widowed with 7 children)

Top: Georgie Helyer with a pedigree champion Texel sheep on their Hanging Langford farm.

Middle: The Rainbow's End Public House on the A36 which has been selling traditional ales since 1898.

Left: Talking of the old days, the three senior citizens of Steeple Langford : From left Violet Green, Doris Foyle and Dorothy Crozier.

Jane Lemon with a fine embroidered box made for the Queen's Silver Jubilee in 1977.

Below: Mrs Annie Witt who for 52 years served Ushers pints from wooden barrels in The Railway Tavern, which closed in 1966.

who also had "the shop" built. There the whole community used to meet. Dorothy, aged 21, was called back from Guide Camp to run the Post Office.

Today Anne Waterhouse, newly arrived in the shop, laughed with me about the mishaps of moving house . . . the loss of half their furniture and a fire in the chimney.

The Langfords have a changing community focus. Building the 18th turnpike on the north bank of the Wylye began the ascendency of Steeple Langford. With the coming of the railway, the centre shifted to Hanging Langford. Now it has returned.

Any Steeple Langford villager would recognise Jane Lemon's new altar frontal. There are the hills, the trees, the trout lakes and the ancient Harrow Way cutting its hedgeline up the steep hillside. A translucent cross completes it.

Jane's workroom was once the butcher's shop. Her designs, colours, stitchcraft and goldwork have gained her a national reputation.

As you approach the church, 20 heads — animal and human — grimace down from roof level. Indoors, it is cool and quiet. There you find Waleran, a 1275 forester boldly outlined in pink, black skull-capped Joseph Collier (d. 1635) with his flat white beard, Mompesson arms, the AD 850 Saxon cross, the 1509 face of Cuthbert Tunstall and the 1904 bellringers' rules. Those rules must have worked. For Langford church probably holds a bellringers' record. Six young men, who were all born in the Langfords, rang those bells together for 50 unbroken years. (They were Henry Ford, William Ford, William Rowden, Edward Down, George Watney and John Watney.)

There's peace and swans at the water's edge in the valley where Paul Knight runs the trout farm in three old gravel pits. In the fourth is Major-General Robin Brockbank's bird sanctuary.

"Fifteen years ago it was a bare open windswept lake," he said. Today, it is ringed by willow and alder, there's a hide and floating reed-covered rafts for the birds to nest on. ("Up to 160 different species during the breeding season").

The 1860 Chilmark stone First School has climbing frames, coloured beanbags and Postman Pat cut-out on the wall. A notice on the door tells of the Mother and Toddler group (Tuesday 10-12). "It's a happy little school," said head teacher Mary Garrard.

She takes some of those 28 children in their bright blue jumpers to youth hostels in the summer. ("Some never go further than Salisbury. It's very exciting.")

Miss Jones was schoolmistress and there were about 100 on the roll when Dorothy Crozier went to school "in boots and white pinafore tied at the back".

Before school, she delivered the milk with a bucket and jug — and was often late.

"Because of TB, I often needed to spend half days in the open air following the sheep on the hills."

When the gypsies camped on the Ox Drove to cut hazel for pegs, and money was short everywhere, the Seagrams at Bathampton gave Steeple Langford children sixpence for carol singing. Dr Topham, rector, gave them "a cake and a few coppers and with two shillings, we were rich."

One can see the tithe barn in Duck Street made from Armada timbers, the fine Manor Houses in both Steeple and Hanging Langfords, and the big houses on the borders . . . Bathampton of the Mompessons, Bellington Manor, and the Pembroke's turretted Little Langford farm.

But Bill Henderson has done the digging. He explained that "Steeple" came from the Staple, a post driven in to mark a Wool marketplace or a ford . . . that the name was first used in 1310 ("Stupelangford") . . . and how the Wirr got its name.

In the 14th century there were 118 adult males. The Black Death cut the population, and "it has taken until this century for the population to crawl back," he said.

The Langfords have always been Royalist. (They probably still are.) A church plaque begins the story of one Henry Collier who, "In ye time of ye Rebellion...was sequestred from ye Parsonage 15 years."

But it was Bill who finished the tale of 1645:

"Mrs Collier snatched up a small glass drinking cup" as she and her seven children were driven out into the snow. Homeless for 15 years, the family slept in a barn and gathered sticks in Grovely wood. When they finally returned to the rectory, (alias Corpus Christi House where Walter Dower lives today), "Mrs Collier triumphantly wore in her bonnet the same little drinking glass."

Two Collier sons fought with Penruddock and were sold into slavery. A Collier daughter wrote a satirical 17th-century bestseller — "The Art of Ingeniously Tormenting."

It was only six years ago, Bill said, that the Rowdens died out. (They go back to the beginning of parish records.) The Thrings are alive and well. They came from Northampton. The Foyles and Earleys survive and Mrs Doris Foyle is the most senior villager.

Of the landowners, the Andrews of East Clyffe have been here for four generations. "I remember when they employed three parts of the village and owned three parts of the houses," said Alan Crozier.

It is thanks to Donald Andrews that Steeple Langford can house its elderly residents. "I sold them the two acres needed for Edgar's Close," he said, "near the recreation field my father (Edgar) had given."

They're strong on cricket, said the rector. There are two football teams too.

But no-one shouts their traditional nickname any more. From 1795 when Rector Sam Weller died in mid-sermon, they were always known as "Die Uprights". Then in 1914 it stopped.

Top: Life in Hanging Langford in the 1930s with chickens clucking around the farmyard.

Right: Derrick James with his wife, Mavis, in the garden of their Railway cottage home in Hanging Langford. Mavis is the oldest indigenous Hanging Langford resident.

Above: Retired farmer, Donald Andrews of East Clyffe, who provided housing for the village's elderly by selling two acres needed for Edgar's Close.

Below: All Saints Church, Steeple Langford, where six local men rang bells together for 50 years.

Laverstock

The Rev George Bull, vicar of Laverstock and Ford, at St Andrew's Church.

Below: The Laverstock Panda appeared in 1969. Now it is virtually grassed over.

Left: Kathy Coles on the balcony of her Downview Road flat. She moved to Laverstock at the age of four and lived in the chauffeur's cottage on The Hill estate.

ONLY IN DOWNLAND names like Cockey Down and Frisky Bottom, where the rare bee orchid grows and intrepid ramblers walk today, will you find an echo of the days when Laverstock was Laferce-stok, an Anglo-Saxon settlement filled with the song of larks.

For today, as Pamela Street puts it, Laverstock is Salisbury's swinging suburb, "where the River Bourne winds in to make its small contribution to the swelling Avon to the east of the City on the far side of Milford Hill".

Its population is 2,766 and though you can still find donkeys, pigs, a bottomless well and dotty grass, you are more likely to see its up-market houses, its bungalows, pebbledash and schools.

At lunchtimes from a phalanx of four schools standing shoulder to shoulder along Church Road, 2,000 schoolchildren spill out. At hometime it resembles a bus station.

St Andrew's School was built in 1888 but St Edmund's (1962), St Joseph's (1964) and Highbury (1974) are new arrivals which the village is slowly digesting.

There is still a tiny nucleus of old-timers who remember the village of 505 in 1911, when St Andrew's School had 30 children and Miss Shergold ("full of rheumatism and rings") boxed your ears ("how those rings hurt"). Children walked five miles to school from Clarendon and "Puddin' Viney" earned his nickname with his bread pudding dinners.

They all gathered recently in Laverstock's last thatched cottage on the green to chat about the old days . . . fishing for minnows with jamjars on a string and tickling for trout on your tummy . . . playing highwayman with the horse-and-cart postman who submitted cheerfully to his hold-up . . . unforgettable real-life dramas like the fire at the Duck when beer flowed down Duck Lane and the boys' chain of buckets which put out the Rangers Lodge threshing machine fire.

"I remember Rev Aldworth, a proper comic," says Archie Cable, carpenter, gravedigger and verger, "waving his arms and legs on his bike."

"His eyes looked different ways when he rubbed his glass eye," says Ernie Norton, at 83, still parish council chairman.

"A good thing cows don't fly," Mr Aldworth said to his wife when a bird dropped something on his cap.

The village was cleaner then than now, even with open ditches, and everyone knew each other.

Laverstock House, the private asylum, was part of the community. Children were sent with bowls to buy "lunatic dripping" from the cook, Mrs Maggs, (5½d a pound). A. S. Rippon of Somerset used to be allowed out to play for the local cricket team. Another inmate could stop dogs fighting.

But the children's favourite was Mr Bouger who supplied chocolate in church and threw ha'pennies and pennies in the river at Six Hatches. "Wrong colour, Sir," they shouted, so he threw in a sixpence.

Tommy Dyer, who in life was wheeled home drunk in a pram, was found to have no coffin when the grave was opened. ("Could the cancer have eaten it away?")

County Councillor Richard Lodge fought to keep today's bus service. But the old-timers remember a fare of 3d return and the first car built by carpenter Mr Kellow.

T. H. Wyatt's St Andrew's church was built "in a twelvemonth" in 1859 (cost £2,353) because the other was "very damp and ruinous". The church hall is in constant use, Jumble Sales £10, Weddings £45, Electricity extra. The Vicar's wife helps at the

Evergreen Club for the over-60s and meals are served on wheels.

The Sports Club has 2,000 members, two football pitches, fishing rights and three bars. Labour Minister Richard Crossman honoured Laverstock by opening its early sheltered housing scheme in 1964. NuScreen publicity provides employment. (So does the Optica aircraft factory at Old Sarum).

There are flying lessons too and model gliders at Old Sarum, Wimpey's the builders are refurbishing the forlorn service houses but lost their appeal to chop up St Probus' playing fields.

Parish meetings wax indignant over litter, vandalism and heavy traffic. Street lights have arrived and with it a speed limit . . . and . . . high on the downs behind the schools' terrapin classrooms, the spring grass is growing over a certain controversial Panda cut in the chalk by uproarious Bangor University students one Friday night.

Elsewhere in the city you'll also find Scouts, Guides and Good Neighbours, Whist, WI and Playgroups. You'll find hanky-panky in the bus shelter, vandalism, and litter as well.

But where Bemerton joined Salisbury in the 1920s West Harnham in the 30s and Stratford in the 50s, this village of one pub and one shop has kept aloof.

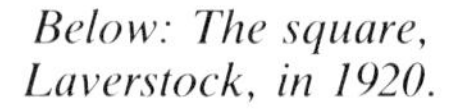

Below: The square, Laverstock, in 1920.

Left: The rooftops of modern Laverstock.

A TISKET, a tasket, a green and yellow basket, I wrote a letter to my love and on the way I dropped it . . . the tiny children sing in Laverstock. So perhaps did King Ethelwulf, father of Alfred the Great. Only it was his signet ring (oval, engraved with his name, two stylised birds, a Staffordshire knot and triangular leaves) he dropped in Laverstock (850 AD).

Nearly a thousand years later, in August, 1780, an unsuspecting William Petty found it in a cart track and sold it to a Salisbury silversmith for 34/-. Lord Radnor bought it from him.

Few suspect Laverstock's ancient roots when they visit it today. Yet it still has its old stone bridge at Milford, where ancient pottery was made, the ruins of Clarendon Palace nearby, flint-and-stone-chequered 17th century Manor Farm and the 1790 "griffins" watermill in the hamlet of Ford. Airmen, of course, revere Old Sarum's flying history.

But Laverstock got a mention in the Saxon Chronicle and its original church antedated Salisbury cathedral.

A mere wattle-and-daub hut with rush-strewn floor, it formed the centre of medieval Laverstock life. There wandering friars preached, proclamations were read and peasants gazed in awe at wall paintings.

In 1410 an indulgence was offered to raise money for the building of a new church.. But by 1853, its walls and roof were insecure. Now Rev George Bull officiates in a mid-Victorian T. H. Wyatt church. Since 1939 it has had electricity, paid for by Archie Cable's whist drives. It cost £60.

Until the Reformation, Laverstock formed part of the property portfolio of prestigious Wilton Abbey. At Domesday, though Odo of Bayeux had just pinched 240 acres, it had a mill, three ploughlands

Above: The chairman of Laverstock Parish Council, Ernest Norton, at home with his cat, Dixie.

Above: Hidden in the forest, the sparse remains of the once-splendid Clarendon Palace.

Below: Duck Lane in days gone by.

Laverstock House, a private asylum from 1841 to 1954.

and was worth £6.

Much Laverstock land had already been given to Wilton Abbey as dowries for young nuns. Fear of the Black Death accelerated the process. More of Laverstock went to the Abbey, some to Wilton's Hospital of St John and some to the Priors of Ivychurch. Panic produced some extraordinary candidates for monasticism.

At nearby Clarendon Palace, today hidden in the forest, the Church and the world struggled for supremacy. When Thomas à Becket objected to Henry II's reforms, nature took his part.

His path from Winterbourne to the Clarendon chapel turned miraculously green — and remained so even in winter's snow. He is still remembered in the name, St Thomas' bridge.

Later kings mortgaged Clarendon. But it remained good name-dropping territory. Edward Hyde (of Hyde Park) held it until Charles II . . . Samuel Pepys (while protesting his innocence) tried to steal its trees for shipbuilding . . . and there highwayman William Davis set upon the Duchess of Albermarle as she left. She didn't frighten easily. He it was who galloped away with an earful of curses, for this "homely dowdy" Duchess had been born Nan Hide, a London washerwoman.

Laverstock had other humble heroes. Rents ranged from "one peppercorn" to "six barbed arrows", courageous William Fawkener paid over £734 in fines for his Catholic beliefs. Thomas and John Milbourne were beheaded by Richard III and parson Francis Bayley got the sack for using the old prayer book.

And, of course, there was poor Henry Burry who lost, regained and relost 150 acres in Laverstock as favourites changed under Edward II.

The marriage of Laverstock (population then 101) to Ford occurred in 1649 ("Though it ought today to have its own parish council," says Richard Lodge, 25 years a councillor).

Milford's celebrity was Henry Fielding, whose "corrupt and shocking" novel Tom Jones was partly written there.

Over the centuries, Albemarles, Earls of Bath and Bathurst have all been Lords of Laverstock Manor. The most notorious High Tory squire of Laverstock, was surely Mr Justice Burrough.

Unqualified barrister and landowner, Sir James Burrough of Laverstock had a predeliction for hanging. His 1822 death sentence on 28-year-old Charles Smith, poacher, outraged William Cobbett who made it a cause celèbre. He rehabilitated him with a second tombstone saluting him as martyr to the game laws, and publicly pilloried "Jemmy Burrough."

Those who knew the gentry in more recent times have nothing but praise for them. They tell how Major-General Cox opened Mill House grounds to the Evergreen Club. Major Byles on The Hill (he of the torn raincoats) halved rents when times were bad. The Cole family got the chauffeur's cottage cheap — and later were allowed to use its electricity.

"First he said, don't use it, then use it once a month. Finally, we could use it all the time," says Kathy Cole.

But the respected Dr Harcourt Coates, whom the Salisbury General Infirmary honours, is less gently remembered here: "We nicknamed him 'Butcher' Coates — he loved to use the knife."

Laverstock changed little from 1801 to 1931. It was a village of 800 and the children helped on the farms, walked to Salisbury on errands and marvelled at the railway and at strangers.

By 1971 it had 3,000 of them. But the new Laverstock holds itself apart from Salisbury, and resists building on the downs or by the Bourne. It still has its ancient pride.

Netherhampton

TUCKED INTO a loop away from the A3094 with its thundering traffic, the quiet hamlet of Netherhampton (50 houses) seems tranquil and timeless.

Its noticeboard tells you where to buy its village history and that the Groves Educational Foundation is being revamped. Nearby there is a pillar box at the farm gate, a bench to EIIR (1952 and 1977) and a plaque on a shed whose door is tied with red binder twine.

"Erected by N. P. Grove AD 1837 to receive Fuel to be given to the Poor Inhabitants of Netherhampton", it says.

There's no shop. A library visits. The pub sells cigarettes. And Rev Bede Cooper's church of St Catherine (1876) which still uses the old form of service, is partly run by laymen like Brigadier Tony Taylor from the White House.

If recently tragedy and controversy have touched Netherhampton and thrust it into the headlines, it comes as no surprise to those who begged for the loop to include the whole village. For traffic rushes past those at the eastern and western extremities. The new red bricks in the park wall point to many fatal accidents.

Most recently, brakes failed and a school coach hurtled downhill into waiting schoolchildren. A 13-year-old boy was killed.

A kerbcrawling gardener stole Netherhampton's plague stone for a rockery . . .

A vast Netherhampton superstore has been thrown out by the city planners.

At least they found no oil when they drilled near Flowerland's bustling garden centre.

And Westonian commercials, Dunns seeds, Overs, and Wellworthy, and the Coombe Hill coach park barely impinge on the peace of the village — any more than the golf club on the hill.

"My Lord Pembroke's Manor of Netherhampton" (Henry Shute's title) had 149 people in 1841. It still has. There are three medieval open fields between the 1550 Race Course and the Roman Road, water-meadows beside the Nadder and the same "Street" once gated against animals.

There you will find the thatched Victoria and Albert pub, ("please park prettily)" the 1876 Church (the third in the village) and the amazing 1720s facade of Netherhampton House, home of Sir Henry Newbolt for 27 years.

The Gauntlett family who made 17th century pipes lived there too, and you'll find a battered stone glove (=gauntlett) they left behind on the gate crest.

But it is Sir Bruce and Lady Richmond who are the most fondly remembered. They'd always send a maid with an offer of help if there was trouble, Marion Thomas says. (Who better to tell you of old Netherhampton? Her mother was a Hayden — and they were there in Tudor times).

Above: Kennedy Smith, the illuminator, at work in his studio.

Right: Marion Thomas, whose mother's family, the Haydens, have lived in Netherhampton since Tudor times, was the first lady church warden. She has just retired after 12 years.

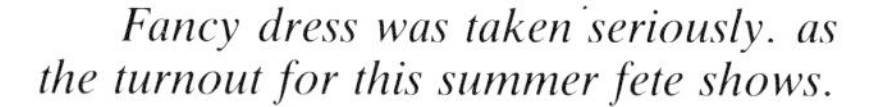

Fancy dress was taken seriously. as the turnout for this summer fete shows.

Above: Netherhampton House, home of Sir Henry Newbolt, Sir Bruce Richmonds and the 17th-century Gauntlett family, who made clay pipes.

Left: Henry Shute, historian, with the original deed for the village school.

Until the war came, she remembers a close-knit village with games in the road ("just a country lane"), paddling on summer evenings and children climbing on the school wall to watch the traffic on Race Days.

She went to the 1840 village school founded by Phillipa Groves, where Miss Clarke was called "Governess" to her face and "Govie" behind her back. It's now a Nursery School. Rector Guy Campbell would call in to see her father after visiting the school and demand a glass of milk straight from the cow.

Henry Shute will show you how Edward Perrett's 2000-acre Pembroke farm was once divided among the villagers. "Copyhold was most successful — like a little communist state," he says.

He admires the layout of the Tudor strip fields, the model rebuilding programme of Sidney Herbert and the long benevolent reign of the Pembrokes. They lent their patronage to many a school prizegiving, and their park to many a Fete. (Behind that redbrick park wall lies the lost village of Washern).

Twenty pounds a year was left to keep Netherhampton churchyard by Princess Alice, Duchess of Athlone in 1966. Her real interest was the flat roadside tomb of her friend, "IMMA GUSTAVA MARIE LOUISE PAULINE EDDA ADOLPHINE ERMINE, daughter of their Serene Highnesses, the Prince and Princess of Erbach Schoenberg, 1901-1947.", a lady with a gift for handwriting analysis and healing hands.

An unassuming man with the glittering skills of medieval illuminators lives in Netherhampton today. "Mary does the chemistry for me," says Kennedy Smith, Fellow (since 1969) of the Society of Scribes and Illuminators, who has exhibited in America and lectured in Australia, been filmed by the BBC and lectured abroad. The village even has an expert on stained glass.

There's no village hall to bring them together. Twice-weekly taxis have replaced the village bus.

"But," says Mary Smith "when the bus service stopped, 30 people offered car rides to anyone who needed them. We may not be close-knit any longer, but when the need is there, the people are there."

And there already more than 2,000 signatures (including Salisbury's Mayor and Bishop) on that petition to move the school bus stop from the spot where Kes Somasunderam was killed last November.

Almost the entire village turned out for the planting of trees to mark the Queen's Jubilee Year in 1977.

Newton Tony

RIDE a cock horse to Banbury Cross to see a Fiennes lady upon a Fiennes horse. Otherwise visit Newton Tony where in a long-lost Manor House that intrepid Puritan lady was born.

On a tablet in the 1844 St Andrew's church is a footnote mention of Celia Fiennes (1662-1741). Between 1685 and 1712, mostly alone, she criss-crossed England on horseback, from Newcastle to Penzance. Her 'Severall Journies' and the nursery jingle keep her memory alive.

The inclusion of an 'e' in Toney (1981 pop: 379) is an emotive issue. So too is streetlighting, homes for young families and the closure of footpaths. The riverbed runs down the not-very high street and there is an annual lottery to guess when the water will start flowing.

Long-ago the railway enabled schoolchildren (like Winifred Armstead) to go to "the Bishop's school". Norman Armstead ran "an individualistic coach service." Today, there's still a bus but the railway cutting is a tip, the station full of hay.

The troublesome "Tony" came from "de Toenye," a Norman knight, says Tony Lyons, who has been researching the village history.

Mud and thatch walls are still a feature of the "little sequestered village" described by Sir Richard Colt Hoare in 1826. West Farm has fine gables and mullioned windows and the Queen Anne Old Rectory, discreetly withdrawn up its long drive, reputedly has ghosts. There lived Rev Phillips, whose daughter "pulled up" Winifred Armstead for not curtseying, and Rev Wright, who "always looked for a salute."

Near the church which the Rev Geoffrey Davies tends from Allington I was introduced to the (doomed) Reading Room. "On those lovely cold tiles, I learned to dance," says Miss Armstead.

Today's social focus is the 1920 Memorial Hall. There's football, badminton and a youth club, a four-village horticultural society, a toddler group, Sunday school and Alec Taylor's summer and Christmas plays. Add to that fun runs and jumble sales, two OAP Christmas dinners and a harvest supper with sherry, soup, cold meats and jacket potatoes.

One may visit Wilbury Park Estate at 15mph and on business only. The 1710 Palladian seven-bedroomed mansion and its grounds still impress though a gale in March felled 130 trees; the October hurricane uprooted another 100.

Dowager Lady St Just is fondly remembered everywhere in her old coat, enjoying bonfires or

Fire at the blacksmith's shop on August 18, in 1911.

Historical novelist Anne Neville (alias Jayne Viney) teaches at the village school.

Winifred Armstead was born in the village more than 80 years ago. Her father was the wheelwright.

Below: The old railway station on the Bulford branch line.

playing musical chairs at the school. Today at Wilbury, gamekeeper Les Toogood still supervises weekend shooting and there are two dairies with 280 cows. But there are no village lads in boots and patched trousers.

"We couldn't even afford pushbikes till we left school," Les Toogood says. The first four cars were unforgettable — Mr Williams' at Manor Farm, Mr Maffey's bullnose Morris, Parson Wright's Austin and the carrier Mr Armstead's taxi. Today all the incomers have cars.

At Hazel Cant's modern village school for five to 11-year-olds, Bernard (one of 33 pupils) showed me the four-wheel-drive car he'd just made. ("The lights work, too").

They treasure their school. Families who have moved away still ferry six children back. But only a handful remember the old school building, burned down one Bonfire Night, which was heated by a big round Tortoise slow burner.

In the 20s, this was a village of floods and fires. Bert and Elsie Daubney's furniture went upstairs every winter because of the water from the overflowing river. Miss Armstead and her mother saw smoke from their pony and trap on Porton Down. Returning, they found their own home was on fire. Les Toogood remembers the excitement as his father carried furniture from the blaze in the three thatched cottages opposite the church.

Through two World Wars and many bad winters, Gwen Razey delivered Newton Tony letters twice a day. The Post Office issued her bicycle and uniform ("a new overcoat every four years"). Railwaymen dug her and her postbag out of a snowdrift in 1915.

"That myxomatosis year was awful, too," she says. "I had to leave my bike at the kerb and hop over all those dead rabbits. They were all piled in heaps together. I couldn't eat a rabbit now, not after seeing what I've seen."

Until the great sale of 1924, Wilbury and the village belonged to the Malets ("very poor, very nice and very caring").

The name stuck to the black and white village pub, with its mossy tiles — the Malet Arms. There, newly arrived, John and Lyn Harrington are set on turning it back into the centre of the village with interesting food and a beer portfolio.

For it's not all nostalgia on the "No Through Road" a mile from the A338. Though few remember riding the swing boats at Trinity Monday Fair in Maffey's field, everyone speaks of today's happy mix with the "whole wealth spectrum and every skill except a thatcher."

Today's Newton Tony has Anne Neville, historical novelist, teaching its village children.

Showbiz glamour emanated from Lady St Just's Wilbury House when they filmed E.M. Forster's "Maurice" there.

Right: A break for tea during the harvest of 1929. From left, Jim Toogood, John Williams, Tom Goodridge, Les Toogood, Jim Toogood and Bill Toogood.

Nunton

THEY tell me NUNNA, a farmer, (not a nun) gave his name to Nunton. The Ebble runs beside the village, its famous watermeadows built by 17th century Dutchmen rising to the chalk downland. Above, Clearbury Ring maintains its brooding watch. "Our dogs don't like it there," they said.

Sir Richard Colt Hoare found "early records silent". He did trace copyholders Fygg (1588), Newman, Lacy, Attwater, Chubb and Bampton. Nunton's first gentry were Botenhams under Henry III, he says, followed by Clarkes, Batts, Buckleys and Radnors.

It still has a feudal feel. Old retainers live in tied cottages. People tell how their forebears swept the road from New Hall to St Andrews' for the Buckleys to drive to church. Peter Tucker remembers stout Charlie Musselwhite, the last old-fashioned drowner, too.

Nunton's different strands come together for the annual fete. Today's mix includes the professionals and upwardly mobile, but there are still farmers, indigenous locals and old folk. The 1972 sheltered housing scheme, the Orchard, "has 22 front doors."

Charlie Ford is the oldest villager. He even went to school in the Parish Room. (1915 directory: Elementary school with residence for 52 children, Miss A.L. Smith, mistress).

Tucked beside the Rev. Robert Hollingshurst's church, it was headquarters for the Young Farmers during the war. Today it's home to the WI, fortnightly whist and children's church workshops.

St Andrews is a picture postcard Victorian church which Bill and Grace Barker keep immaculate. It began as a Chapel of Ease for Downton. The south chapel has 12th century work, there are pews still labelled "free" and Victorian monuments to Buckleys and Batts. There's also a 1982 tapestry medallion for Prince William embroidered by Vice-Admiral Sir Charles Hughes Hallett.

But the village is proudest of Ernest Fray, organist for 62 years. A plaque near the organ marks his astonishing service record (1908-1970).

Today Nunton has two remarkable artists — Kathleen Muir, Royal Academician and landscape painter who began long ago "by scribbling on the nursery table", and Michael Payne with his sought-after vivid World War II aeroplanes in oils. ("Models without the mess," he says, laughing).

Nunton House (1660?) with its fine ceilings, panelling and staircase, was built, they say, by a merchant whose bride insisted on living within sight of her mother. He obliged, but turned his house to face the other way. The delicate white 1700 pavilion in the Dutch garden is listed, and the mighty ironwood tree is one of only three in England.

The Radnor Arms ("Patria Cara Carior Libertas") under Richard Penny has a tiny red snug with a dart board where mud on your boots is still acceptable. Next door, it's good food, gleaming brass cartridges and a smart clientele. (No mud).

This was once the domain of John Henry Chown, Flour, Corn and Offal Merchant. "Big, hot-tempered and boisterous," he was landlord, grocer and baker.

When cars arrived, Chown's bread van doubled as school bus, farmer John Martin bought a bullnose Morris truck and Lord Radnor drove a sparkling black Ford V8. But ducks still walked safely down the middle of the road and the tug o'war team pulled weights over the Martin's elm tree.

The copper beech near the rectory was planted by the WI (founded by Lady Radnor) for Queen Elizabeth's coronation. They used to meet at Nunton farm to can fruit and tomatoes and make baskets, and

Above: Nunton's three smiling services . . . John, Bridget and Peter Tucker in 1942. Peter still lives in the village.

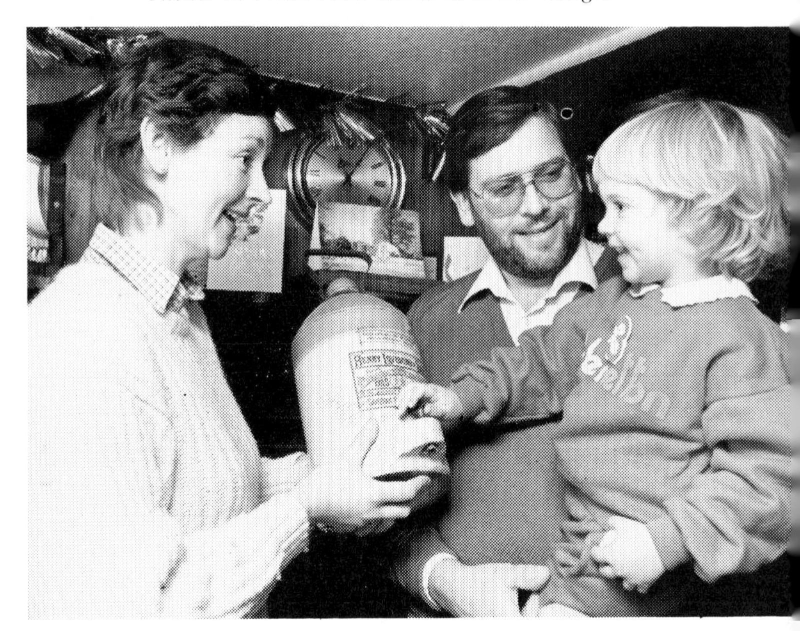

Above: Publicans Lesley and Richard Penny with daughter Louise with one of the old Lovibond stoneware bottles that decorate the bar of the Radnor Arms.

Right: Former schoolmaster Michael Payne, with his book on wartime planes and their markings.

Bill and Grace Barker, who keep the church immaculate.

there were memorable expeditions to the Albert Hall.

Nunton still produces corn and milk, as it used to do. Where once the Gullivers, Vincents and Martins farmed, only the Martins survive. "The area I farm employed 27 families in 1957," says Peter Martin. "Today there are seven."

Farmwork was hard but it was much more sociable. Gangs gossiped. Harvest tea was carried up to the "hiles" (stooks) in cider bottles with socks over them.

In the war Nunton had rationing, a Home Guard and an ARP post on Bodenham Hill. Norman Race remembers his father, armed with a whistle, firewatching from a shepherd's hut - and the mice runnning about. The Luftwaffe dropped a bomb behind the Radnor Arms and killed a hare above Odstock. On VE night, Longford Castle sent a jeep to take old Mr Tucker to the bonfire at Clearbury Ring.

Nunton had 44 houses in 1947, says Peter Tucker, former postman. Now there are 96. Traffic has arrived and so has the commuter.

But they still remember Captain, the last carthorse, and can show you the shed for the village bier. Here estate life survives — and in Nunton they like it that way.

Above: Nunton in 1929.

Organist Ernest Fray with choir members in 1956. He was organist for 60 years and his daughter still lives in the village.

Below: Peter Tucker, ex-postman, with his favourite painting of a corner of the village by local artist Kathleen Muir.

Odstock

CLIMB from Salisbury ("with its quaint houses and beautiful cathedral") over its southern hills and you will "come to another hollow in which is the old-world village of Odstock."

This tattered article in a long ago glossy magazine was one of Dora Parrett's treasures. She had many. Until she died aged 94 in January 1988 she was for Odstock a unique link with its unsophisticated past."

True, she couldn't quite remember Iron Age man in Clearbury Rings, the descent into the valley for water or the Saxon ODO who built his STOCK(ade) beside the Ebble. Hence the name.

By Domesday, Brictic held the £10 manor. Tristen and Diana de Vere Cole who live there now are only its fifth owners. But Mrs Parrett (born Compton), the youngest of 11 farm labourer's children, remembered agricultural Odstock, under the Radnors.

Her widow mother scrubbed the school at night and made the morning fires. Girls took pride in their clean white pinafores and walked to Salisbury to shop.

They learnt drawn-threadwork by making three-cornered aprons for Miss Snelgrove the teacher and went to church three times on Sundays.

The Odstock band was led by blacksmith bandmaster Frank Feltham. For the harvest service it marched from the crossroads. Best of all was maypole dancing with Miss Miles, the rector's daughter, instead of scrubbing the school on Saturdays.

Odstock today is justly proud of its renowned hospital on the skyline, once an American camp ("but they couldn't start building till the corn was cut in 1944").

Peter Ford, the builder, descendent of tradesmen who were bastions of Odstock, says after the US troops went home, his father, Percy, flew their flag "on a scaffolding pole beside his verandah on July 4 until he was 91."

As undertaker, Percy wore a "sheeny greeny black suit", employed 50 men for 50 years from his Dickensian premises and at 89 was still digging graves singlehanded.

Then, horse tassels were ironed and brasses gleamed for the annual ploughing matches, and reputations were made at Longford Castle flower shows.

The Duke of Windsor came to inspect a piggery, a child died when her pinafore caught in the millwheel and Odstock cabbages were famous.

Lads like Peter watched breathlessly as the four Felthams, blacksmiths, heated and hammered and poured water on the steel "tyres" they bound to

Above: The fabric designs of Georgina Von Etzdorf have brought the world of high fashion to the village.

Above: Builder Peter Ford makes a wishing well for the village fete.

Left: Odstock band in the early 1900s. The bandmaster is Frank Feltham.

Above: 1940: Odstock's contribution to the war effort — corn grown on the tennis courts at Odstock Manor. Mr Parrett is the man in the hat on the left.

Below: The Ford Dynasty — Percy (carpenter), Bob (plumber), Charlie (bricklayer), Les (painter) and Dick (electrician and carpenter).

wooden wheels. He remembers every gesture . . . and the smells and shouts of "Come on you old Divil" from the farrier shoeing in his leather apron.

The Supernatural has its part in Odstock's story. Not just because an unsuspecting Ian Root as a schoolboy saw Cromwell's ghost in Glebe House. Jeffrey Wyatt, schoolmaster, never forgot how he saw Cromwell's picture and exclaimed, "I know that man. I saw him in my room last night." Nor because skirts rustle in the Manor House.

It is the curse of the Gipsy Queen which keeps St Mary's church unlocked. Two men this century have died within a year of locking it. For in the churchyard, its briar rose trimmed, but arching protectively round the cracked headstone, is the grave of folk hero Joshua Scamp. ("*May his Brave Deed be Remembered to his Credit Here and Hereafter*").

Some travellers' children attend Odstock school today. In 1975 they took part in Mrs Sue Finnis' typically ambitious project to recreate the Scamp story. They even made benders. Their musical portrayed the long oiled curls, Sunday smock, top hat and yellow muffler of the gipsy hanged in 1801 for his son-in-law's crime.

It was the carousing at his graveside each September which dismayed the rector. But that was nothing compared to his horror when, discovering Joshua's thornbush ripped out, gipsies ransacked the church, cut the bell rope and overturned the tombstones.

Mother Lee cursed the rector, churchwarden, sexton and a pair of turncoat gipsy brothers . . . along with anyone who locked the church door. To dire effect.

Today Odstock produces few cabbages and no hooleys in the graveyard. Its population, including the hospital, is 528. Children walk in crocodile up to the Manor House and the fete is held on the lawn. No-one sells saucepans or clothes pegs outside the Yew Tree Inn, or tethers a tinker pony nearby. There are expensive cars instead.

But what about the bustling, burgeoning enterprise in the Manor house barn? For that is the home of the Georgina Von Etzdof label worn by Princesses, Duchesses and fashion leaders the world over. Here "mild English eccentricity" has become megamoney.

If you look through the windows you can see a 60 foot print table and workers in brightly daubed overalls. Upstairs (Weds and Sats) you can buy clothes and accessories — handkerchiefs, scarves, screen-printed ties and shirts, dressing gowns and silk-lined mohair coats.

Left: Odstock village in days gone by.

Right: Dolly Parrett, aged 93, in front of Compton's Cottage, where she was born.

Pitton

THERE ARE still a few people living in Pitton who remember travelling to Salisbury on the early morning bus with the milk churns clanking and calves for company on Market Day.

They include Brian Talbot, Parish Clerk since 1969, whose grandparents lived at the Silver Plough pub, when it was Ivy Farm. (There Eyres and Co built wagons — one still preserved at Paultons — ran a smithy, off-licence and shop). There's also 99-year-old Mrs Bessie Stevens, Norman White and tolerant Jack Judd, opposite the Post Office, whose barn door serves as village notice board.

It is on that door you will read of the Tennis Club, the social club, the coffee morning at the 30-strong primary school, the Drama Club, Gardening Club and activities at the 1970 Village Hall.

But you will hear little of the gypsies who came on Mondays to sell bootlaces and clothes pegs and buy rabbit skins. Or the Socials in the old village Reading Room (a World War I hut from Larkhill). There villagers did turns ("Alf {Puzzle} Collins told wonderful old jokes in Wiltshire dialect"), The Bubbles Concert Party performed, and there were dances and games.

A highlight of the year was the annual outing to the seaside in a motor coach ("In earlier days it was a horse-drawn wagon ride for the children to Pepperbox Hill or the Forest").

At Christmas time, there was a children's party at Clarendon House ("You were collected at the cross roads, remember?").

Tom Collins' horse and waggon went via Clarendon to Salisbury. Lewis White ran buses to Salisbury and also had a horse and carrier business ("If you wanted him to do some shopping, you put a newspaper or card in your window and he would stop and collect the order"). Those were the days when the bus stopped for passengers wherever they were, and seats all faced inwards.

Bell's coaches from Winterslow were the opposition and still serve the village today ("An adequate service, but nothing after 5.15 or on Sundays").

Modern Pitton is a compact community of 500 cupped in a waterless valley, five-and-a-half miles east of Salisbury. Newcomers have been welcomed and assimilated and it has been likened to "one large estate". Only the crooked tombstones recall Pitton names — Whitlock, White, Collins and Seaward.

Modern brick and pebbledash cottages vastly outnumber the mossy thatch. Until the 60s there were 12 groups of thatched farm buildings — now there are only two.

The county council took part in this historical massacre, demolishing its own Manor Farm and barns, to make space for new houses.

"It was a truly rural community until 30 years ago," Brian Talbot says, and quotes with a wicked glint a departed Pitton clergyman: "We may have lost a squire, but we have obtained several would-be ones."

Above: Brothers Brian and Donald Talbot in front of the Silver Plough, once Ivy Farm, the home of their great-grandparents. Brian is clerk of the Parish Council and Donald the chairman of the local cricket club and British Legion.

Middle: Ivy Farm (now the Silver Plough) in 1892 when it housed a shop, off-licence and Eyres and Son, wagon builders. The baby in front is Kathleen Mills, Brian Talbot's mother.

St Peter's church.

A panoramic view of Pitton.

Above: Jeanne Judd of Coldharbour Farm, looking after the village notice board, which also happens to be her barn door.

Left: The old bakery is now a private house.

Certainly today there are homes for doctors, bank managers, army majors, and even a former editor of "The Field", but few that young couples can afford.

The public footpaths show that instead of working in Porton, Boscombe, Wallop, Salisbury and Southampton (as now), the good folk of Pitton found employment in the neighbouring woods. All the footpaths lead, not to the open downs, but to where the woodland crafts (spar making and hurdle making for sheepfolds) were done.

It was along the top of the downs that old Alexander Pearce, builder and blacksmith, set out at 6 am from Winterslow to his apprenticeship in Pitton. And Brian Talbot's father — the first Pitton lad to go to the grammar school — was allowed out 15 minutes early in winter because of his one-and-a-quarter hour walk home through Clarendon woods.

The old folks tell of brawny dockers from Southampton who came to Pitton at slack periods to saw tree trunks for Eyres and Co in the sawpit, with hand cross-saws.

The muddy puddle near the church was the famous Amers Pond where you watered your cattle and horses. There's also the famous Pitton Harbour — despite the dearth of water!

They remember the excitement when water and electricity arrived in 1938.

Here Methodism has deep roots. Pitton Methodists first met in a small cottage at Slateway in 1801. It was stalwarts like the Briants, Pitts, Frys, Webbs, Baughs and Whitlocks who helped build the present 1888 chapel.

Today's energetic rector Rev David Hart travels from West Dean to East Grimstead, Farley and Pitton Church. In his flint and stone St Peter's, a brass plaque reminds us of the days of our "soveraigne Lady Quene Elizabeth" (Edward Zouche, d. 1580).

But a more macabre reminder of the old days in Pitton appeared in 1958. While digging out a septic tank in the front garden of "Westfield", workmen uncovered a skeleton from about 1800 BC — a contemporary of Stonehenge.

Rockbourne

ROCKBOURNE is a picture postcard village on the Hampshire-Wiltshire border. Thatched cottages fringe the village street. To reach them, you cross tiny bridges spanning the little brook beside which artists plant their easels.

Here history is right on the surface. But in 1942, farmer Tom Porter was digging out a ferret and uncovered a notable Roman Villa, which today attracts tourists by the coachload.

Mrs Brixie Jarvis, who helped Morley-Hewitt's excavations, is still there to share the mood of those heady days.

If you visit the church by car, you use New Road (around 1800) and park in Lady Studd's Manor Farm. Its history began before Domesday. Medieval farm buildings cluster around the whitewashed manor house, and from there parishioners clamber up a steep incline to church.

What a church! There's a 13th century cinqfoil arch (to match the one in the farmyard) tucked inside a Saxon one. There's a grating over the blocked-up Western door where a fox once sought sanctuary from the Wilton hounds. He fared better than Thomas à Becket.

There hang the threadbare regimental colours of Major General Sir Eyre Coote (d 1783) who helped Clive conquer India. Like Cleopatra's needle, his monument, and his nephew's, rise above his old home, West Park.

Rockbourne Church is full of Coote memorials, a Coote chapel, a Coote gift of a 16th century triptych and a family vault.

There's a 1685 carved chest, a Charles II coat of arms in a diamond lozenge, a 15th century font and a hotch-potch of re-used stonework around William Johnson Yonge's 1893 window (51 years as rector).

The rectors of Rockbourne were powerful men, for the Lord of the Manor lived elsewhere. None more so than this Rev Yonge. Two cottages and a Village Hall were built in his honour by his maiden daughters, who saw that the village dances lived up to its "Temperate in All Things" inscription.

Today's rector, Rev John Hathaway, lives in Damerham and looks after the spiritual needs of the four villages of Western Downland, Whitsbury, Rockbourne, Damerham and Martin.

Shrinking iron bands on to cart wheels in the early 1900s.

China restorers Judy Wood and Philippa Craig, making good other people's damaged treasures.

Bill Mouland, 89, the oldest native of the village, visits the Old Rockbourne exhibition in 1986 at Western Downland school, with his wife Lilian, his cousin Kitty Read and teacher Jane Little.

Above: Teacup in hand, local historian Andrew Winser and Rev John Hathaway, Rector of Rockbourne, look at photographs of bygone village life at the school exhibition.

Left: Brixie Jarvis, who helped discover the Roman Villa in 1942, holding a Roman pot found in 1967 with over 7,000 coins.

School statistics tell the population story. In its 1851 agricultural heyday, Rockbourne had 83 children being educated and a further 91 who should have been. The present school began with 86.

As numbers began to drop, Rockbourne and Damerham schools were federated under one headteacher five years ago. Today the schools thrive under Mrs Judith Sheppard, but a recent survey by the children showed only nine of its 110 pupils come from Rockbourne. It now serves the same four villages as the rector does.

"Rockbourne today is predominantly elderly," says Mr Hathaway. "It is a sad thing, too, that without a post office here, the old agricultural workers in council properties with no transport have to leave at the end of their lives."

"What changed Rockbourne was the coming of the tractor," says local historian, Andrew Winser. He has interviewed the survivors of the old families and written up the village, the life of the shepherd and carter, the story of the church and the houses. Given encouragement he gives a splendid impersonation of Lady Coote, who like Jane Austen's Lady Catherine de Burgh, longed to control the parson.

Better still (even in pouring rain) he will walk you round the village and show you, like old friends, the history through the houses. First the 15th century cruck cottages ("and do you know what copyhold was?"), then the fine 17th century yeoman farmer's houses with yard and outbuildings.

Today the 17th century cottages are again single dwellings, for celebrated hospital consultants and retired professional military men.

But don't ask Andrew Winser about modern Rockbourne. The outline of the celtic fields, the deerpark behind the manor and the brick-making at Sandle Heath (formerly Sand Hill Heath), these are the things that make him glow.

"West Park was built by a Rector with 14 children. An unburied dead woman caused a boundary dispute."

Andrew's wife, Jill, clerk of the parish council with an electoral roll of 325, will tell you of community life — lunches on first Mondays, the WI and the loss of the British Legion. Notable weekenders include Sir William Van Straubenzee, MP for Wokingham.

Rockbourne has known Sir Walter Raleigh's son. The father of the first Earl of Shaftesbury chose to send his children to Rockbourne to escape smallpox. In the 1830s agricultural rioters (fortified by Rev Yonge's homebrewed cider) burnt Manor Farm's threshing machines and marched on West Park. Lord David Cecil lived at West Hayes and Augustus John held noisy parties at the Rose and Thistle.

But for centuries Rockbourne was on the road to nowhere in particular, a little agricultural backwater. And that's why it's so unspoilt. So far.

Shrewton

PEOPLE have lived in Shrewton for 3,000 years. One of its Bronze Age residents is in Salisbury Museum. It has seen highwaymen on the old coach road to London and a flood so great in 1841 that 30 houses were destroyed.

It's a village of little bridges and new estates, new hard sharp outlines tucked in everywhere among the authentic cottages, the walls of flint and cob, brick and stucco, the thatched and the manor houses.

Opposite the friendly "Catherine Wheel" pub, like a grimy roadside beehive stands the sinister 18th century lockup ("one of 11 in Wiltshire"). For the morbid there are ancient burial mounds and a gibbet site.

There were once seven tiny settlements in this, the Till Valley — Shrewton, Maddington, Rolleston, Homanton, Elston, Orcheston St Mary and Orcheston St George. Orcheston and Shrewton (Winterbourne Shreveton) survive. In the days when it was owned by the Sheriff, Shrewton boasted three vicars. Today, with a much larger, changing population, (1981 pop 1,680 — and still growing) there's one.

But the Reverend Stanley Trickett's enthusiasm is infectious. He tells how Shrewton Methodists, Baptists, Catholics and Anglicans are presenting a united front, worshipping together once a quarter, running a joint sunday school.

"We all worship the same God. Separating into our different corners is a nonsense," he says. Mr Trickett's is a story of House Groups, and healing and of the exciting pilgrimage he has taken four times to the Holy Land ("It brings your whole faith and the Bible to life").

There's a lot more going on, from the Silver Band to the Mummers, the Day Care centre to the Playgroup, drop-in coffee on Wednesday morning, cricket and football, Brownies and the rest.

From Rollestone Church, with its chequered walls and wooden turret, founded by the Knights Templar, you look down on the squelchy riverbed and the clustered houses below. Maddington Church has been closed, but St Mary's is down where the action is.

Right: Five senior residents relive their memories: Standing, Harold Cruse (left) and George Withers. Seated, Mrs May Hall (left), Mrs Nellie Wiles and Eric White.

Below: Shrewton's little flint church, St Mary's.

The famous 18th century stone lock-up.

skyline is Rollestone camp, still used occasionally as a prison. The 1987 prisoners were welcomed at St Mary's. Two of them spoke powerfully at the morning service. One was married there. And Shrewton was grateful for their work, cleaning up litter and tidying the graveyard.

Salisbury Plain stretches in every direction. And the army is a big employer. But there are four pubs and two garages, pig farms, racing stables, builders (assorted) and local employment for 25 at the Hall's laundry. There's a village policeman, nurse and doctor, with a physiotherapist wife.

Only a handful remember the days of 14 shops and six pubs, when it took all day for a child hit in the eye by an onion to get to Salisbury by carrier's cart (No Ladies Upstairs).

Now the 150-pupil school straddles the High Street, Lloyds Bank looks like a dolls house, there's a British Legion and a Social Club, splendid climbing frames at the recreation field, "Hair so Fayre", newsagent, post office, grocer "and don't forget Billy Baxter our fantastic butcher."

Get the old-timers together and they'll tell you of old Phyllis Chick a long-ago eccentric whose brain had been affected by childhood measles.

There were the "big families" who lived in the big houses, often with families who worked for them for generations. The Smiths lived at Rollestone Manor, the Haywards at Maddington Manor. Shrewton recently lost its well-loved Lieutenant-General Sir Robert Hinde, from Shrewton House, but Lieutenant-General Sir Rohan Delacombe, former Governor of Western Australia, still lives at Shrewton Manor.

There were the Chants, a large village baker family who organised fancy dresses, concerts and village entertainment. "Especially Phyllis and Ivor," says Amy Hall. "They ran everything."

Old Ollie Withers supplied the village with coal. Two bakeries made bread and lardy cakes for the camps. Today George Withers had time to chat, (his son ran the dairy) and few remember Annie Wiles pushing her three-wheeled handcart.

Harold Cruse was the special constable at a time when you walked the village and knew everyone you laid eyes on.

"Everyone left their doors unlocked," Amy Hall explains. "Many doors didn't even have keys.

"You never saw parents meeting children after school," Frank Matthews added. "If a policeman boxed your ears, it was 'serve you right'."

Another masculine activity was collecting horse manure for the allotments, many of which had a chicken pen and pigsty. Rabbits were plentiful at harvest time, when the men would stand and wait with sticks ("You could get two for 6d from old Mr Cooper").

Many of today's old-timers remember the coming of electricity in 1932 and how it showed up the dusty corners — and the damp. There were bad throats when the stream was coming up or going down, regular floods until the bridges were widened and boards to keep feet dry when going to church.

But no-one is alive to describe that dramatic flood in January, 1841, when the Till rose seven feet six inches, claimed three lives and led to the building of those whitewashed cottage clusters a year after "that awful visitation".

Above: Shrewton in the early 1900s . . . friendly societies celebrate Trinity Sunday with the village band.

Below: The Catherine Wheel offers roadside refreshment.

Sixpenny Handley

THE SCHOOLCHILDREN'S red sweatshirts at Sixpenny Handley tell you than Saxpena and Hanlega, two Saxon Hundreds joined in 1244, gave the village its name. But the tanner (deceased 1980) is remembered nonetheless in a shop called "Alf a Sixpence" and "Sixpenny Bits" accessories from Guy Parker's leatherwork factory.

The 1873 school building belies its modern teaching under Mrs Anne Hodgkins. On a Tuesday morning I found mothers in the classroom playing educational games with their children. Nearby the incubator was full of ducks eggs and the walls showed experiments with pontillism.

Still a "working" village with few weekenders, Sixpenny Handley lies in a valley close to the Wiltshire-Dorset border, and includes eight satellite hamlets. Its population estimated at 880 in 1985, is growing fast. Homes range from a double decker bus through mobile homes and executive estates to manicured Chapel Farm.

Thirteen miles from Salisbury and ten from Blandford, local shopping is good and you can park outside. People travel from the Midlands to patronise the Clarke's immaculate slaughterhouse (flower arranging also a speciality) and nearly everyone delivers. Even the dentist will treat your toothache in your kitchen. Newcomers receive an eight-page "Welcome Leaflet".

Light industry flourishes. There are three pubs, and though the village is growing fast, it now has a planning "envelope" to control its sprawl.

The face of today's village is in part due (like the village hall) to the devastating 1892 fire which began in the wheelwright's shop. Generous clothing parcels arrived and some parishioners donned three waist-coats.

In St Mary's church enjoy the heavy stone-roofed porch and the carving of "Christ throuned in glory" on the wall. The Abbess of Shaftesbury prosecuted Hanlega's first known parson, Nicholas-de-Longespée for chopping down trees. Nonetheless in 1292, he became Bishop of Salisbury.

This was until the mid-1800s a village of smugglers. Isaac Gulliver, wealthiest of them all, married the Thorney Down innkeeper's daughter in St Mary's in 1768. The Thorney Down pub became his HQ and, all over the village, cellars concealed tea, tobacco and brandy.

It was a poacher's village, too. In the churchyard you may read on a slab: "*This stone was the cover of the tomb which was removed to afford space for the enlargement of the church in 1879. When deerstealing was prevalent, the deerstalkers used to remove it to place in the tomb the deer they had taken, till they had an opportunity to remove them.*" Village children used to dance round it in hot weather so flies did not attract attention.

Despite transportation and flogging, sheep stealing kept families fed. "Ghostly" corpse bearers reported at night on the Burley road turned out to have sheep's carcasses on the bier.

In 1830, there were riots: ("Such fun, the men's bustin the 'chinery and a-burnin of it in the yard.") Victorian "justice" was dispensed. Some fled.

One hundred years ago, most people in work were in farming. In 1962, Dorset Council set up six smallholdings as starter farms here. Today, their dairies, beef and sheep are doing well. The bigger farmers have arable fields, too.

Above: Countryman Dougie Judd recollects a long and hard-working life.

Below: John Curtis (right) chairman of Handley Parish Council, at work with Kevin Easter in their village upholstery business.

Right: Norman Clarke, with his son John, check the fresh meat hanging in their spotlessly clean slaughterhouse.

Above and right: The main street in Sixpenny Handley in the 1930s and today. After 50 years, the Roebuck Inn remains a landmark.

Photocall outside Handley Council School in 1913.

Left: St Mary's church, with its Norman porch, protects worshippers from the weather as it has done for 800 years.

Tales of the old days, like the poetry of William Barnes, come easy to Dougie Judd, who ran the defunct Silver Band. Son of "Carrier and Jobmaster, Frank Judd" (calves on the tailboard, parcels on the hood), his boyhood included nutting and scuggy-hunting "hooping and hollering through they woods".

At the November "Woodmen's Derby" at Farnham, "strappers" would buy their "lugs" in the woods. Until March "when the sap rose", in copses with names like Scrubbity and Mistleberry, they cut hurdles and spars and sorted faggots for the baker, birches for firewood. "Everything were used in them days" (the same held true of the family pig). Haymaking began in June, and harvesting followed.

In those superstitious days, it was a "Cunning Woman" who cured an epileptic boy. His mother split an ash sapling, passed the boy through it thrice and bound up the tree . . . a pigeon's heart stuffed full of pins was stuck up a Deanland chimney . . . and Old Cutty Hobbs chased the first spring butterfly, shouting, "I got to catch he, then my enemies can't do me no harm the rest of the year". No-one would work on Sundays.

Councillor John Curtis, upholsterer, who started Handley's Scouts at 13, was at the famous street lights meeting ("They're making my plants grow at night!").

They may be more sophisticated in Sixpenny Handley today. No old men wonder how to blow out "the candle in a bottle" as they did when their lights were installed. But much of the old-fashioned spirit remains.

Teffont

BEST-KEPT village in 1973 and 1983, with its Chilmark stone houses beside the "Teff" trout-stream and its thatched bus shelters topped with birds, Teffont didn't need its sprinkling of snow to make it pretty.

Artists seek out turretted Teffont Manor and the man-made lake. Garden-lovers visit the four-acre grounds of Fitz House built by 17th-century wool-merchants.

This tiny strung-out village with its ancient rivalries and big divide at the Black Horse Pub, only became one parish in 1922.

So 262 people have to maintain two churches — in Teffont Magna ("the upper village") the plain Norman St Edward's and in Teffont Evias, the more ornate St Michael and All Angels. There under glass is kept the exquisitely-illustrated 1956 WI history of Teffont.

Until his death in July 1987, undertaker Ronald Lever was custodian of Teffont history. His house was filled with watercolours, Roman coins and Saxon pottery. He treasured his 1741 vellum Teffont account book.

"Teffont Magna was mostly tenanted — a real working class village until after World War II," he used to say.

In those days village boys would chant: "Upper Teffont Candlesticks, Lower Teffont Belles, Chilmark Lousy Dirty Slums, Fovant Pretty Girls," and the even more Wiltshire: "T.E.F.F.O.N.T./ You may beat eggs but you can't beat We/There are trout in the river and snakes in the grass/Teffont — Magna — Evias."

It was Ron Lever who pulled out a Chinese shrub and found a rare ninth century Anglo-Saxon carving, and who earned 6d for a driving a calf to Salisbury.

His mother walked to Tisbury to have her teeth pulled and walked straight home again. "During World War I, we spread mashed potatoes in milk instead of butter on our bread," he said.

Vic Goodfellow ("still a wonderful pig man") was also taught by Mrs MacPherson at the school (closed 1936). ("My golly she was strict — but what a

Charles Merrifield, who has lived in Teffont since 1930, waits at one of Teffont's two thatched bus shelters, renovated for the Queen's Silver Jubilee in 1977.

1936 - The last children at Teffont school with the Rev Keatinge-Clay, before closure.

Ronald Lever, the late village undertaker, by the old sheep wash at Spring Head. Sheep once brought prosperity to Teffont. Few are found there today.

Fitz House in Teffont Magna was built by 17th century wool merchants.

Sir Edgar and Lady Keatinge at home at Rose Cottage, Teffont Evias.

Catholic knowledge!"). None of them saw the sea till 1925.

Bill Newbury used to tell of Curate Cooke, "a man to be feared. He made him lie down against the schoolroom door to keep the draught out," Bill said.

"But Curate Collett was a dear old man. Not a rich man, either, yet he bought us book prizes. So did a Miss Walker. I still have my 1919 Best Infant prize," Ron Lever said.

On the walls of a barn by torchlight I read: "Harvest 1946, Manor Farm, Teffont (its' agricultural heyday) August Rainfall 5.51ins. 4 fine days. September rainfall 6.52ins. 6 fine days. Terrific gales sweep ears of corn off the straw and beautiful crops vanish and return to Mother Earth. Bread is rationed. May Almighty God bless Manor Farm and all who work within its circle and forever spare their eyes from such a dreadful and affecting sight. W.F.C."

This was the farm Lord Bledisloe bought from the Pembrokes. "He repaired the cottages, gave them concrete floors and gave each villager a virginia creeper," says Ron Lever. "The Autumn colours were beautiful." He also started the flower show in 1919 — still an annual excitement.

Two forward-looking farmers followed — William Fisher-Crouch and Alistair Pitcairn. Teffont farming is still changing, says local District Councillor, David Parker. There are now no sheep, only three herds (including Tom Thatcher's Chianinas), and a lot more arable.

In the heart of the village ("on Charlie Giles' farm") plans are afoot to "forge a link between town and country." John Vining is inviting the public to Spring Dairy to watch the Friesians being milked, the pigs, sheep and goats.

The most colourful — and talked about — change was that of John, a Fisher-Crouch nephew who, until he opened his Wessex Shire Park in April 1987, farmed 4,000 sheep.

The first season brought 25,000 visitors to Teffont to admire his shaggy shire horses back in harness, the parades, displays and cart rides.

"Last year's harvest was great fun," says Rosemary Webb, "cutting the corn with binders, using horses to pull in the sheaves and threshing in the old way."

Sir Edgar Keatinge, former MP, whose son is now squire of Teffont Evias, had misgivings. Rural industry like furniture-making in the beech woods attracted him more. "Picture the litter and the traffic," he said.

Mercifully the village hardly noticed the first year's tourists, and in the second year financial problems threatened the future of the shire park. Teffont house prices, though, remain high.

Lady Nepean started a gardening club to bring the new Teffont together. There's a Golden club, too, a part-time Post Office, pub, stud farm and three noticeboards. Buses appear, and organically-grown fruit and vegetables are sold from a barrow.

Deprived children come for holidays in the Old Malt House. A blacksmith, mechanic, electrician, wheelwright and builder ply their trades.

But like the floods which raced through the village in July, 1982 ("water over the pews") and September, 1984 ("a trout on Rowland Ling's lawn") change is coming.

Let's hope they retain the stories of Jinny Foster, their witch, and tenth child, Mary Humby. She went to church attached to a sprig of myrtle, "so the rector could not claim her as a tithe."

Upavon

IF you were born there, you are an Upavon Jack, short for Jackdaw. (The oldest Jackdaw is Gaffer Yeates, now that Mrs Ball has moved.) If your parents were Jackdaws and move away, your status drops to Tree Jack. But if your parents were Jacks and you were born within sight of the church tower (with its jackdaw nests) you become a True Grey Pole, Tower Jack.

Upavon (called Oppravene in the Domesday book) has always been a little special. It has a ghost called Warren. William I kept it for himself as a Royal Peculiar. It had a palace and Henry II signed documents there. A grassy hump behind the 1175 Norman church hides an unexcavated priory linked to the Abbey of St Vandrille-Fontanelle. High on the edge of the ranges is Casterley Camp, an Iron Age hill fort. There they found four skeletons, antlers, Roman coins and a Roman farmstead.

Today's village of 1,500 is segmented. Away out of sight on the Everleigh Road is "the camp." Locals enjoy the golf course and sports facilities, but the glorious operational days of RAF Upavon, birthplace of the Air Force, are over. The Museum is named after the legendary Lord Trenchard. It was from here recently "they organised the refuelling of flights to the Falklands."

The council estate began as RAF married quarters. It too, stands apart. It has the 1957 primary school (140 pupils) under Mike Chislett, headmaster. "Nearly 40 per cent come from RAF Upavon," he says. The estate has some splendid vegetable gardens, and its own methodist chapel.

Passing Sally Lewis' pottery in the Old Bakery (and the layer-cake yew tree), you reach the old village in the valley. In Chapel Lane is the 1838 Cave of Adullam, home of the Strict and Particular Baptists. At the Pewsey end is the caravan site and on the hill the Fairfield estate.

But the village that grew up as a staging post still centres on its busy intersecting roads and the fine square. The Antelope Inn (Wadworths) faces its Ushers rival, The Ship, with the crenellated church tower behind.

It's a tumbled mix of old and new, big houses and sheds, modern infill and mossy thatch. The 1911 Village Hall is being refurbished "to draw the village together."

Over the Coomer's corner shop door is the head of Henry Carter, a long-ago grocer. Opposite is the Post Office which moved from "Sparrows Perch." There are brash signs on Jon Wildman's Racing Garage and discreet ones on Marshalls factory. The roadside Jubilee mural "was done by the lady who smocks children's dresses in the little Victorian school."

Two views of Upavon from St Mary's church tower taken in 1900 (below) and 1988 (above). The basic layout has scarcely changed.

Retired poultry farmer Charlie Andrews Triangle House. Charlie was born in the Antelope Inn just across the road.

The head of Henry Carter, grocer, above the door of the corner shop.

Right: A pair of Gray Pole Jacks survey the view from St Mary's church tower. George Buckland (right) is chairman of the Parish Council and Steeple-keeper, Geoffrey Stevens is a parish councillor.

Long-time Upavon residents, Jim and Sylvia Chisman. Jim's family have lived in Upavon for nearly 250 years.

The Central Flying School staff at Upavon in 1913. Lord Trenchard is third from left in back row.

Hardship hit Upavon in the 1800s. A Penny Bank was started in 1877 (interest — a halfpenny a year on 1/8d). Desperate families held a public meeting in 1874 to ask for allotments. Women leazed wheat in the fields, made dough and took it to the baker's. There men pulled out the coals, washed out the ovens with wet sacks and then put in the loaves.

Three generations of Fullers were village bakers and the last, David, is still baking at Barry Wookey's organic farm at nearby Rushall.

Whit Monday was a big day in Upavon. In the 19th century, the village band led the parade which ended with a feast in a cart shed. "Until the war on Whit Mondays, we had greasy pole fights, a five-mile race and coconut shies in Birkler's meadow," says Sylvia Chisman.

One drunken Victorian schoolmistress wore long curls and galoshes and called her assistant "article 68". But True Grey Pole Tower Jack, George Buckland, parish council chairman, knew respectable days in the old school. He's a school governor, winds the church clock and has rung tower bells for 53 years.

Jim Chisman's family have lived in Upavon for 250 years. He was godson of the legendary Captain Howard Alexander with his beagle pack.

The boys used his dog biscuit tins to make rafts ("one on each corner") and the village girls cooked in them. His toboggan seated eight and the boys used to smoke secretly in his cartshed. Children played tops, hopscotch and hoops in the square and went carol singing with lanterns.

It was Mrs Alexander ("tall, slim, a perfect lady") who presented Charlie Andrews with his school prizes 64 years ago. His spare time was spent rabbitting up on the downs, in the days when Upavon supplied London and Southampton with 73,000 rabbits a year. Gutted and hung, they'd be packed 40 to a box, and taken to Woodborough station daily.

In those days the Ship was a real local with scrubbed tables and patrons like Old Shepherd Davies and Shepherd Woodrough.

"This was a real country village and I knew everyone," Charlie says.

The High Street at Upavon around the turn of the century (from Geoffrey Stevens' collection).

West Dean

ASK A STRANGER about West Dean and he will tell you it is bisected by the Wiltshire-Hampshire border and that a nuclear convoy crashed there in January 1987.

Sensational headlines ill prepare you for this tiny tranquil village (1981 pop: 290) approached through over-arching leafy lanes, with its thatch and cottage gardens, whitewashed station and ducks on the green.

On the Romsey Road is the thriving 100-year-old sawmill, East Bros, which employs 40 ("excluding the family"). Andrew East, great-grandson of the founder, took over a workforce of seven in 1966.

Today you dodge busy yellow lifting trucks to wander through mountains of pallets and logs, dwarfed by sheds where lasers are used, sawdust and offcuts become paperpulp and imported hardwoods are stacked roof-high.

Just beyond is the Royal Naval Armament Depot, Dean Hill. Inside the hill, we are told, the Navy stores its arms in a complex of tunnels built about 1938. I saw no nuclear convoys, Polaris ballistic missile warheads or depth charges. Flat roofs and the red-brick housing in Hillside Close is all the village knows. ("Don't ask us what's inside Dean Hill. At least it stopped the developers and kept the village unspoilt.")

The Singer (sewing machine) family which owned and employed West Dean as agricultural workers are gone from Norman Court, but Church Farm (appropriately owned by the Parsons) flourishes in the heart of the village. It has a magnificent 16th century buttressed tithe barn.

Hampshire and Wiltshire share Dean's historic monuments as well as its pub.

An early British Fortified Mound stands at the top of Rectory Hill. It was levelled off and recycled as a bowling green by the Evelyns of Dean House.

There's the (107 foot by 32 foot) Roman Villa found in Hollyflower field in 1741 and first excavated by Rev G.S. Master. They went on digging (with the 'help' of the railway cuttings) until 1873 when they covered it up. Painted wall plaster, hypocausts and baths were found. One four-foot floral tessellated pavement went to London in the 1840s. It was later on display at the Golden Cross pub, Charing Cross.

"This 'Villa Urbana and Villa Rustica' was part of a whole chain of villas down the river," Stanley Gledhill says. "Take East Dean, West Dean and Holbury at Lockerley."

It was on the ruins of John Evelyn's 1601 Dean House, on which he became an expert, that he built his bungalow 32 years ago. Underground tunnels were found. Village children told him of lanceheads they'd seen long ago when exploring with candles in jam-jars.

Though no-one has pinpointed for certain where in 1131 Waleran built his Hall at 'Duene', Gledhill's discoveries leave no doubt that the Evelyn mansion with its orangeries was to the west of the old church (demolished 1867).

The disused 1333 flint Borbach Chantry is all that's left.

Above: Bill and Peggy Parsons and their ancient barn at Church Farm.

Right: Landlord John Sharp whose Red Lion pub spans two counties.

The East front of the vanished West Dean House.

Boating at West Dean during the 1982 open day.

If you visit it unaccompanied, you'll probably miss the gravestone marked 'Also J.T. Cooper, brother of the above' to the man who was hanged at Winchester for his part in the 1830 Fordingbridge Swing Riots.

Gilbert White the naturalist was curate here in 1755. The Beauchamps in the village and on the graves are traceable to 1333.

Once inside the chantry (kept locked) the monuments to the Evelyns eclipse other celebrities.

To your left as you enter is the painted alabaster and marble 1627 memorial to the builder of Dean House. Sir John and his wife are kneeling face to face over a stool, showing every sartorial wrinkle in robe and ruff. Below them facing the altar, with unpainted eyes, are eleven children (three with beards) and some with broken noses.

To the right of the door is the white bust of Elizabeth Tirell who died in childbirth in 1629 and there's a dear little 1641 brass to six-year-old George Evelyn.

At the altar, massive, on one knee, eyes upraised, complete with cherubs, pillars, urns and doors covered with yards of golden copperplate writing, is lifesize Robert Pierrepont, who died in 1669, and is commended for "such Patience and Passive valor in cutting off his legg as was to Admiration".

Benefactions of money, food and clothing are written up in gold on a great blackboard over the door. In 1684 Sir John Evelyn provided £20, Edward Thistlethwayte added £10-9s-0d in 1730 and Thomas Baring in 1873 a further £60 to succour the poor of West Dean.

Stanley Gledhill has excavated more than the foundations of Dean House. Sarah Evelyn, he will tell you, was disinherited (with a 5 shilling legacy) when she disobeyed her stern papa over her third marriage. One George Evelyn had the valuable national monopoly for gunpowder from 1526 to 1603. Another George died with debts of £7000 ('quite a sum in 1636').

And he will leave you with throwaway remarks on Dean's maypole and its windmill, the bankrupt canal and the last residents of Dean House — French nuns who were forced to leave because of "crudeness and incivility" from the canal navigators.

Above: The entrance to the Royal Naval Armament Depot at Dean Hill.

Above: Andrew East of East Brothers Timber, who have recently celebrated their centenary.

Left: Local historian Stanley Gledhill outside the Borbach chantry.

West Dean is a pretty village with a station, says the Touring Guide. With its tiny population, its good communications make it something of a post-Beeching rarity. Two bus companies call. Houses cost a lot.

The railway station has lost its oil lamps. The 20-lever frame signal box (extended for English China Clay at West Grimstead) went to a collector in 1980.

In 1947, when Dick Hann arrived as a signalman ("controlling trains with a series of bells") West Dean had a station master, clerk, two porters, lamp man and three signalmen.

Steam trains were running, people listened for the big brass handbell and Mrs Hansford came out of her cottage to open the Frenchmoor Lane gates.

Dick saw ex-army vehicles, which had been auctioned in Bentley Wood being loaded into wagons, birch twigs sent to Manchester for vinegar, and logs and coal going to the fuel-hungry North. Sheep from Romney Marsh arrived by train to winter at Dean, there were mares "with foals at foot" from Tytherley stud and Mrs Winterton's goats would hop obligingly into the guard's van.

Then a railwayman's wife cooked on a range, had an earth closet and went to bed by candlelight. But at least there was always boiling water to unfreeze the garden pump from the steam trains in the siding.

Then in the '60s came diesel. No smuts on the washing — and a working timetable no-one could believe possible.

There are fewer trains today, few Wiltshire accents, and the part-time post office, like the village school and Methodist Chapel has closed. There's a fine 1868 church (cost £2,500) in the care of the Rev David Hart, who has for 18 years tended four parishes.

It's a novelty at the Red Lion Pub to order a drink in Wiltshire and drink it in Hampshire. But for some mixed loyalties are a mixed blessing.

Kathleen Parsons has known Dean and its parish council meetings a long time. The boundary has, she says, been on the agenda "as long as anyone can remember".

Years ago St George's Hall, she says, was a busy milk factory, "always awash with water". Cheese was made in the loft and there's a tale of a long-serving donkey who took the churns by cart to the station, alone.

Agricultural West Dean had a butcher, grocer and shoemaker's shop and cows on the green. Mrs Reynolds kept the post office, which included Mr Warry's forge.

Above: Kathleen Parsons in front of her home, Yew Tree Cottage.

Left: The floods of 1960.

The line-up at West Dean's village school in 1924.

Dick Hann, signalman from 1947 to 1980.

Her versatile son Carl is a village legend. He returned from the war to replace Mrs Beauchamp's horsedrawn cab with a taxi and become village undertaker, mechanic, purveyor of electricity and petrol. He charged radio batteries, too.

"We had much more freedom as children. You could be gone for hours with a picnic and no-one worried."

Lessons under formidable Mrs House in her black dress and walking stick meant white pinafores and long desks. The tuning fork was struck on the high iron fireguard.

There were Methodist outings with tea and a scramble for (unwrapped) sweets in the grass on Pepperbox Hill and a thriving Band of Hope. Everyone enjoyed the charabanc outings "with the hood pushed up or down according to weather."

Clouds of white dust rose from the untarred roads up Dean Hill as long-ago racing drivers ("like Frazer Nash") tested their cars.

Postman Stanley Fry, her father, delivered letters . . . first on foot, later by bike (parcels tied in front). He it was who brought medicine from Whiteparish dispensary and collected for the Pig Club and the Infirmary League 'which took the burden out of being sick.'

There are many tales told of the Great Flood in October 1960. It was the night before Harvest Festival, Peggy Parsons says.

Cottagers' children were brought up to the farmhouse in a tractor and trailor ("water was over their Rayburns"). A disbelieving morning-after hostess went back to bed when she saw her dinner party debris floating by.

In 1977 in Dean, they sewed yards of Jubilee bunting, they have harvest suppers, a prayer group, a drama group and a wine circle. There are fetes and bazaars and a host of activities (including a surgery) in St George's Hall.

Only the boundary question still divides. Even a referendum didn't resolve it. Some say Hampshire clears the snow faster. But the church is in Wiltshire. (Before 1473, there was an ancient All Saints church which wasn't).

There are two refuse collections, two library vans, two education authorities and some families can choose where to vote. Who will build them sheltered housing?

The Domesday Book name 'Duene' meant quiet and sheltered. Today it's still a caring, sharing village. On both sides of the frontier, they speak with pride of "our publicans" John and Vicki Sharp from the Red Lion who take a pensioners' lunch on Thursdays to people stuck at home.

An old view of the village green.

Right: The level crossing at Dean Station.

Whiteparish

WHITEPARISH (which began as Frustfield became Alderton by Domesday and Whyte Perysshe by the Reformation) lies tucked in the hollow below Eyres Folly on Pepperbox Hill.

In the centre of this busy village with four pubs, three shops, its own health centre and policeman, the grey-shingled bell tower of All Saints Church overlooks the bus stop.

It's a fine church in the care of Rev Daniel Gooderham. It contains a gruesome St Barbe family memorial window with worms wriggling out of skulls, an 1854 east window, a fine Rigaud painting by Peter denying Christ in the Saxon chancel — and massive Norman pillars in the nave.

Lying between Roman Winchester and Norman Salisbury, Whiteparish has grown into a village of 1,000 people. Some years ago, they united under George Alford to stop N. R. Trickett's intensive residential development.

Now they're united in pleasure at their new health centre. Though the long-serving Bastons (husband and wife) have retired, there you'll find three doctors, a nurse, a health visitor and even a dispensary.

Progress? But Whiteparish still has its saddler and harnessmaker, its cobbler, its thatcher and its versatile postman who doubles as school cleaner and helps at the pub.

The ecclesiastical and civil boundaries of Whiteparish don't coincide. But then it has known many incongruities — Hindu temple and pre-Reformation nunnery and now a medieval chapel used as a chicken house. Colourful characters sprinkle its history. Local writer Brian Woodruffe describes it still as a "village of personalities."

Nineteen years ago, the late Rev Roger Keeley, newly arrived, used to cycle out to take communion to the shy recluse, George Eyre.

Eyre lived, as his family had done since 1633, in delapidated, disintegrating, crescent-shaped Newhouse, piled to the ceiling with copies of "The Times." Today, his nephew, George Jeffries, is restoring the 1619 mansion.

Two old sisters who lived in Brickworth House in the 1900s used to leave food out for the mice, but today Charles Blackwood, at the same address, shares his fine pool and grounds with the village Scouts.

Both Cowesfield and Broxmore Manors were split after World War II. Retired butcher Headley W. Hammond remembers the squire of Cowesfield and his lady attending morning service, while the servants stayed at home and prepared lunch.

The maids had to wait until evening to attend church, and in an interesting variation on the courting game, the village lads would wait for them on the triangle green, then go into church late and bang the door to draw attention to themselves.

There were once three chapels in the village. Only the Methodists survive. In their schoolroom a plaque records the work of lay preacher George Hayter, whose great grandson still lives there.

Hayter's Evangelism began after he recovered from a serious illness and fulfilled his vow to give his life to the Lord. So successful was his preaching that, in 1904, local thugs set upon him as he walked home from Redlynch and threw him into Newhouse pond.

James Lynch was a 17th Century Yuppie. His fine brick house, "Lynches," still shows the oval outline where the self-made man planned to put his coat of arms. But the College of Heralds didn't agree.

He suffered the further ignominy of a court case in Salisbury, where he was fined for using the term,

Above: Sid Pegrum, man of many parts, on his morning round as Whiteparish postman. Sid is also village school cleaner and barman at the White Hart.

Below: Rev Roger Keeley, vicar of Whiteparish 1968 to 1987.

Below: The view from the churchyard, looking up Dean Lane and Bunker's Hill in Whiteparish.

Below: Jack Hyde has been village saddler in Whiteparish for 61 years. He started work for George Till aged 13.

"Gent," after his name. In those days of social immobility, your betters intended you to remain in your place — peasant, yeoman or gentleman.

Lynch's 1705 will is in the vicar's possession. Records show a man by that name founded the first village school for boys in 1639. The unfortunate girls were neglected until 1746, when Anne Hitchcock of Cowesfield left them £10 a year for reading and needlework!

Today, apart from its primary school, Whiteparish has an Eductional Foundation to help bright village children with money from the rent of 33 acres.

For many years the foundation received no income, and it was the young Roger Keeley, who had scandalised an old lady by digging the garden ("in the nude," as she told half the village, though he only took his shirt off!), who traced the heirs of a wealthy landowner in Ireland and collected the arrears.

The parish boundaries are vast and include exquisite rural scenery, the subterranean water reserves which supply Southampton, a Chinese-run mushroom farm, discreet builder's merchant and an electronics firm.

In leisure hours, there's a WI, Garden and Flower clubs, Pepperbox Players doing amateur theatricals, Youth, Friendship and Badminton clubs, playgroup, toddler group, Cubs and Scouts.

Here where William Swayne set his 1934 biography "Parson's Pleasure," you'll still find gypsies cutting hazel in the Gatmore Woods.

Long ago, they say, wayfarers along the road from Salisbury to Winchester, used to rest at Whiteparish. Today's motorists don't even slow down as they brush the kerbside cottages.

Below:
Vera Fortune in the village Post Office at the age of 80. Though now officially retired, she still comes in to help out. A labour of love, she calls it, having worked there for most of her life.

Floodlit All Saints Church.

Winterbourne Stoke

STRADDLING the A303, its population 177, its cottages ranging from flint, cob and thatch to "the finest council houses in the country", Winterbourne Stoke is "a politician's dream", says Colonel John Price, churchwarden.

"Everyone here is in work," he says, "and people still care." There's a pub, church and garage and a doctor's surgery in a private house. At the Wild West Fayre you buy plants from a Lord, and play darts with an Appeal Judge in a Mexican hat. Its bridge appeared on the first record sleeve of Steel-Eyed Band.

St Peter's Church has a beautiful outlook, a Jacobean pulpit, two Norman doors and the remains of an hour-glass for long-winded vicars. Les Rose's Dad borrowed the church steeple ladder to climb down wells in the 1936 drought.

No-one minded when someone read the wrong church lesson, but mention the demise of their village hall ("the showpiece and envy of all, built by voluntary labour") and you touch a nerve.

"It left a bitter taste in our mouths," say those who saw it go.

The land was given by Quaker Banker George Alexander, who once lived at Manor Farm. As well as a ghost and Arnold the butler, he had a Great Dane called Derek, a grey and green parrot and most of the village on his payroll.

The hall's profits went to maintain four retainers' cottages. In 1950, the hall with its full-size billiard table was sold for £1,300 to "renovate and put flush loos" in the cottages.

There are at least four of the old families left, people with fine Wiltshire voices who knew it as a compact little village with a school and full-time vicar, two grocers, café, butcher and greengrocer. Sheep were driven to Salisbury along the Devizes Road.

These were the children who carried four o'clock tea to the harvesting men ("boiled bacon, basins of vegetables tied up with cloths and stone jars of tea"). Mr Waters and Mr Barnett in jockey cap, clay pipe and gaiters met daily on the corner.

The Village Outing, free for children, went to Weymouth. Mrs Lockyer took the money, there was a pint of prawns and a cream bun for tea and the monkeys behind the pub in Ringwood smelt dreadful.

"We usually bathed by the fire on a Saturday. But for the outing we bathed on Fridays. We had syrup of figs in the bath that night. That meant no unscheduled stops for the charabanc."

Daisy Barnett was the 21-stone strength of the village. Unqualified midwife, she delivered every child, laid out the dead and "despite awful legs" delivered the post from Longbarrow roundabout to Scotland Lodge.

Above: Church Street looking towards the A303.

Below: Village midwife and postlady, Daisy Barnett and husband Mark, on a charabanc outing to Weymouth in the 1930s.

Right: Pat Gillingham (left) and Myrtle Hiett, the midwife's daughter, have lived in Winterbourne Stoke all their lives. Pat's husband, Sid, once the travelling butcher, started life in Shrewton.

The High Street in the early 1930s. The shop in the foreground is now the filling station on the A303.

Above: church warden, Col John Price, outside St Peter's Church.

Left: District Councillor Doug West stands alongside today's busy A303 in front of The Bell Inn, where he was born.

When a firework exploded in John Mallett's hand, it was she who walked beside him to Shrewton. Her daughter Myrtle Hiett is still on call in a a crisis.

Her father, who paid ½d a week to go to school, left school at ten to scare crows with a blunderbuss.

"You could set your watch by him," say Doug West and his sister Pat. He'd arrive at the Bell Inn at ten-to-ten for his nightly 2d pint. "He'd take the chill off with a poker."

Sid Gillingham was a butcher who cut meat from the van as he went on his 12-mile round. Now 63, he lives in an 1841 flood cottage.

Among his treasures is a dog-eared copperplate account book (1921 hire of a horse, cart and van: 10/-a day). He'll brandish a five-foot long 1902 "humane killer" and tell you how three-year-olds would beg a piece of suet to gnaw, pigs heads were in demand for brawn and roast cheek, and 1/6d bought you a henge for faggots.

"Mince the henge, add breadcrumbs, onions and sage, roll into balls and roast them. Beautiful," says his wife Pat. "Nothing like today's.

In the days when Dorothy and Ernest West were filling stone jars with beer before breakfast, the Bell Inn was usually full of young jockeys from Druid's Lodge Racing Stables, slaking their thirsts in their pub.

But "Wintreburn Stocke" is far older. St Peter's at Domesday was worth 60 shillings and the Lordship was held by Edwarde of Saresburie, standard bearer to Henry I. Priories owned it and nobles like Lord Ashburton, the Chedworths, Howes and Kellows.

To the north lies the Coniger, an earthwork containing round barrows, where they farmed rabbits in manorial times.

Cromwell used the church as a stable, a servant was sent to Australia for watching a fratricide (the weapon a horseshoe) and eight were burnt in their beds in 1819.

Don't overlook the 1574 Customs of the Manor. Here you are reminded how to divide your "arrable" into three "feilds" (sow two and leave one "sommer fallow"). They also plotted the route the "Parsonage Dung" should follow, which was thoughtful . . .

Winterslow

A VILLAGE of independent smallholders, says author and broadcaster Ralph Whitlock of Winterslow, where he lives.

Here, he says, "the spirit of the old peasant commoner of England ... lingered longer than in most places ... its inhabitants being noted for their zeal and their humour."

The history of Winterslow is peppered with the astonishing. Perhaps they needed their humour. Like its lion attack for instance.

If you visit the Pheasant Inn on the A30 turnpike and ask nicely, you may be shown an ignominiously hidden Barrington Bramley painting. It shows the moment in October 1816 when a lioness attacked the Exeter Mailcoach.

The horse survived to become a fairground exhibit, the passenger "brushed" by the lioness went off his head. A 1984 postage stamp recalls it. So did the essayist Hazlitt.

Three ancient cedars on the field known at the Pleasure Green are all that survive of Winterslow House, which was burnt to the ground the night after a party in January 1774, which included theatricals in the barn.

Lady Mary Fox dashed into the fire and rescued her baby, Henry Richard Fox, while the young gallants took bets on which beam would fall next.

The baby who became 3rd Baron Holland gave Winterslow the land for its infant school, and London society some delicious scandal.

The fire drove the Lords of the Manor away. Rectors ran Winterslow instead. Norman Thorne, local historian, has a special affection for the astonishing Brodie dynasty (37 years as rector and a host of famous children).

Peter Bellinger Brodie's son-in-law succeeded him (1804-1840), one Matthew Marsh. He kept fashionable palates in Holland House, London, supplied with Winterslow partridges, live eels, trout, sides of bacon, honeycombs, wild ducks and the famous local truffles.

One of the big houses — Old Lodge — once used as a bombing range on Porton Down, now has only its pets' graveyard intact. It became in 1871 the home of the memorable Major Robert Poore. He it was who gave the villagers their unusual independence and dignity.

A soldier and Anglo-Saxon scholar, he turned Winterslow into a community of smallholders, controlling their own affairs on the ancient tithing system and owning their own land.

He did it by buying Coopers Farm (189 acres for £1,500) in 1892.

He sold off 77 acres and split the remaining 112 into 47 smallholdings from a quarter of an acre to 16 acres.

"In those days, labourers didn't buy land," says Norman Thorne. Poore allowed 39 subscribers to do just that over 15 years at five per cent interest.

The Land Court managed the financial affairs and provided mortgage funds right up to the 1960s.

So, thanks to Major Poore, by 1914 Winterslow was a colony of independent smallholders with an expanding population, when everywhere around it was falling.

Poore's self-governing system continues. Horace Moody is one of the four Land Court members who still meet "occasionally in each others houses."

The Land Court houses, which now fetch £75,000-plus, were built for £100 from the chalk by a professional Winterslow mudwaller.

The holes dug became water tanks, the flints they found went into foundations. Winterslow was now a

Above: Local historian Norman Thorne by the Victorian post box in Livery Road. Behind are the pair of ancient cedar trees that mark the site of Winterslow House, burned down in 1774.

Winterslow Village Hall Murals show highlights from its history. Below: A mural showing a Truffle hunting expedition. Bottom: The great fire at Winterslow House in 1774. The figure on the right is the statesman, Charles James Fox.

village where men worked for themselves.

They cut hurdles and spars and cribs in the winter ("You can't cut wood when the leaf is on.") They had their crops, cows and pig. There are still hooks and salt patches on farmhouse kitchen walls from the bacon curing.

Small wonder the village band, under George Thorne, bandmaster, were happy to walk the four miles to Old Lodge to play carols on Boxing Day. ("And Robert Poore gave them 10/-").

Mrs Poore not only visited the village school to select likely girls for service. She set up local spinning and weaving centres.

Winterslow has links with the Nelson family who only sold Roche Court in 1920; with Hazlitt, the essayist, who adored the spot and Thomas Boulter, the highwayman, who reputedly haunted the Crooked Billet.

The falconer to Edward III lived in Winterslow and had to bring him his claret at Clarendon Palace.

They found flint mines here older than anywhere else in England, round barrows, Saxon cemeteries (many headless skeletons), Roman busts and Iron Age farms.

The name (carried to New Zealand by one Brian Taylor in 1861) means "burial mound" (OE: Wunters Hloew). Unsurprisingly. It's an archaeologist's dream. Recently investigations into a "long barrow" revealed a Roman amphitheatre.

And we ought to have mentioned the Annetts, Yeates and Judds, the Thistlethwaites, Mompessons and Earls of Upper Ossery.

For it is an extraordinary village, even today.

Below: The famous Lion attack on the Exeter Mail at the Pheasant Inn in 1816, shown on a postage stamp issued by the Post Office in 1984.

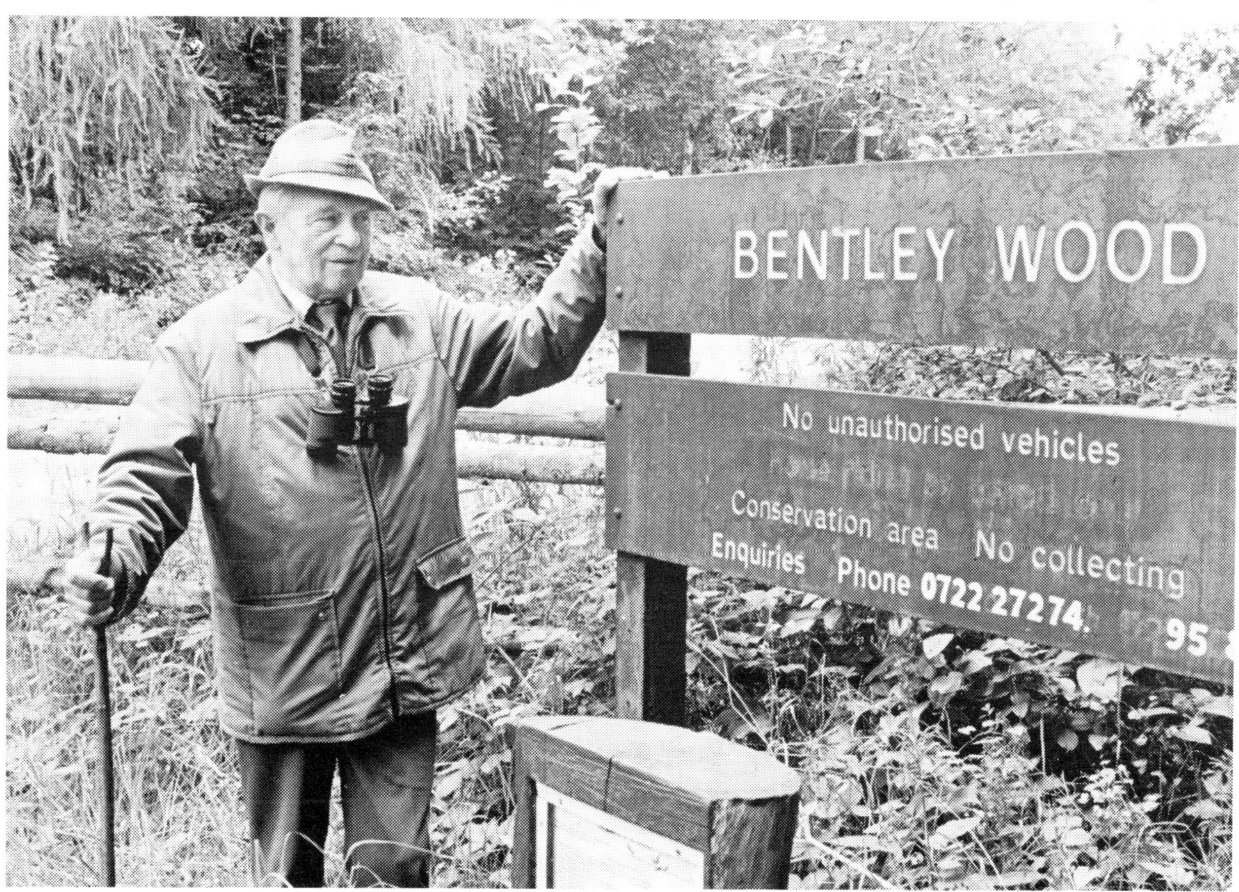

Author and broadcaster Ralph Whitlock at Bentley Wood in 1985.

Whether you've lived in Winterslow for one year or a hundred it's your village if you are living here now, says Rev Clive Cohen, rector.

"We have a strong supportive society of about 2,000 people," says Reg Titt, chairman of the parish council.

"It's a singular village," says Horace Moody, farmer.

"I couldn't remember what it was that felt so special," Mr Cohen says of his return to Winterslow after four years. "It was when I walked through the door of the church that I remembered — it was full of prayers."

Now he speaks glowingly of a village that's "very alive, full of lovely people in whom the ecumenical spirit is growing".

This includes the Methodists, Baptists and the Gospel Lifeboat Mission where Rosalie Keel, postlady, serves as secretary to the 25 followers of 19th-century evangelist Albert Shears.

Lying on a 500-foot high ridge, Winterslow today includes several hamlets as well as West, Middle and East Winterslow.

Only recently was the Shripple anomaly ironed out — it used to be part of Idmiston. Firs Road has been the spiritual responsibility of Winterslow for over 30 years. Yet it was from Winterbourne civil parish it hived off, to become the newly-independent Firsdown.

Sprawling pear-shaped Winterslow is tucked up against Hampshire on the southern edge of the Plain with magnificent views north across the Porton ranges and south as far as the Isle of Wight.

It includes several once-large estates like Old and New Roche Court and Middleton Manor where the munificent Lady Colman lived. Shortly before her death she rescued Bentley Wood from development for posterity.

A major Roman road cuts through the parish, to say nothing of 32 miles of footpaths and "green roads", and outposts like Lopcombe Corner.

No high street binds it togther but there are shops where you need them, pubs in strategic positions and two coach companies to serve the village.

There is much that is unusual here. There is the ancient truffle-hunting family of Collinses, a maker of meteorological instruments in the erstwhile Rechabite Hall, and clusters of families (sometimes three generations) living cheek by jowl.

There are even inexpensive properties for first-time buyers — a Wiltshire village rarity.

This bungalow, now called Arc En Ciel, was a Winterslow weaver's shed.

Above: A pair of original Land Court houses in Witt Road.

Below: The Lions Head, one of Winterslow's three pubs.

Rosalie Keel - a postwoman with a Mission. Rosalie is the Winterslow auxiliary postwoman and church secretary of the Gospel Lifeboat Mission.

Winterslow has semi-urban developments which serve as dormitories for Porton, Boscombe, the Wallops, Salisbury, Southampton and even London commuters.

Community energies seem endless and the list of youth and adult activities cover pages in the parish magazine.

Winterslow's high position ("We are on a level with the ball on the cathedral spire") makes it a snowtrap in winter and creates a water problem. The independent villagers handled this with characteristic self-reliance.

In 1934 they began selling five-shilling shares in the Winterslow Water Society. This paid for a deep well near the butcher's shop, where you can still see the original pump house. No more stagnant water from underground household rainwater tanks.

In 1935, it was appropriately Major Poore's daughter, Nina, Duchess of Hamilton, who turned on the taps. From then on, the emergency water cart journeys to St Thomas's bridge or Dean became part of history.

Water pipes still run through Winterslow fields unmarked on the deeds. The DIY water supply worked for a generation but today they are on the national grid and (as elsewhere) they dig up the roads to lay their pipes.

Today many of the early institutions pioneered by the smallholding generation are inadequate. The village hall was built in 1927 before most people needed parking. The recreation ground doubles as a school facility, but needs enlarging.

In the 1950s the village had about 1,000 people but four pubs, two churches, three chapels, two Friendly Society halls (one now a table tennis club), parish hall, five shops, butcher and two bakers.

The village has its ancient charities, Thistlethwaite, Curtis and Poor Folks (one of them looks suspiciously like an attack of conscience by a lady who had pinched some common land).

Everywhere there are signs of small entrepreneurial activities — from garages to gardening, baking to building.

And everyone appears delighted with the conversion of the barn from which the theatrical Foxes watched the fire of 1774. A man who bears the old Winterslow name of Shears has turned it into a fine modern house — with a FOX and Actors mask on the gateposts. As a reminder . . .

Left: John Jones of J.I.P. Jones (Micro-Met) manufactures micro-meteorological instruments in the Old Rechabite Hall, pictured below.

Woodford

ON THE WALL of All Saints' Church, Middle Woodford, there is a plaque in memory of a domestic servant who gave her employer 60 years' devoted service.

It is not as impressive as the fine lettering and gilt on the list of prebends since 1220, including one Robert who became Anti-Pope Clement VII in 1374 — or the baptismal register dating back to 1540.

It is not as important as the brass to Gerard Errington (died 1596) who built the first Heale House.

But it reminds one of the centuries of unsung godfearing folk who worked the land, their crafts or in the big houses and kept the peace in the tranquil Woodford Valley.

There are, of course, three Woodfords. "Lower Woodford has the pub, Middle Woodford has the Church and Upper Woodford has the shop," they used to say.

Today Upper Woodford has "The Bridge" pub, Col Bailey's clocktower but no shop. There's a woodcraft centre where the smithy stood.

Oldtimers tell of a bridge in Middle Woodford near the church "where we used to cross to Salterton and The Crown at Netton after church on a Sunday night. We nippers gave 2d to the landlord's black dog. He took it indoors and brought us lemonade and biscuits on a tray."

Bootlaces, sweets and paraffin you got from Mr Dear at the Post Office, clothes pegs from the gypsies (who paid 2d for a rabbit skin).

Schoolchildren gathered posies on May Morning, leaving one at every house. Lower Woodford once had a shop and Mummers came from Quidhampton at Christmas.

Those were the days when you went to work on a slice of bread and lard from the pig (salted by Thornton, baker at Netton) and took tea out to the men haymaking in the fields.

You stood and watched as sheep were driven to Wilton's Thursday fairs, scrabbled for the handful of coppers Dr Brown threw over the school wall as he drove past from Amesbury and watched your mother cook potatoes in a string net and boil the bacon with the cabbage.

"You don't get stuff today as you did," says Alfred Phillips, the old Special Constable, describing the annual emptying of the household "pit" and manuring the allotments.

Your rewards came at the Village Flower Show in Heale Park (third Wednesday in August). Woodford honey was famous.

There were roundabouts from Fordingbridge and sports for young and old.

Heale House was a major employer. The Hon Louis Greville's generosity was legendary — a joint at Christmas, a children's post-Christmas party and allotments for the village folk at 1/- a week.

He built the 1901 Middle Woodford Reading Room-cum-Village Hall where Arthur and Beatrice Moody perfected their memorable "Hole in My Bucket" turn.

The valley was not always tranquil. The builders of Stonehenge must have dragged their great Sarson stones that way. It was on the footpath from Winchester westwards.

And in medieval days, with the Bishop living in the Manor of Little Woodford (now Court House), King Henry II at Clarendon and the cathedral at Old Sarum, the Woodford Valley must have been the hub of the local universe.

Its biggest moment came when Charles II, on the run after the battle of Worcester, stayed with

A group of locals enjoying one of the regular charabanc outings organised by The Wheatsheaf, in the 20s. The young man on the extreme right is Alfred Phillips, pictured below with his sister.

Life-long Middle Woodford residents Alfred Philips and his sister Freda Kerley with the Woodford Cross and All Saints Church.

Heale House, winner of the Christie's Historic Houses' Association Garden of the Year award in 1984.

The faces of young Woodford children from the village primary school, the last school in the valley.

Katherine Hyde, widow, at Heale House. No-one told on him, though he rode about freely.

Present-day villagers (no longer primarily agricultural) prize its tranquil beauty. "There weren't even fences on the downs until after the war," they tell me. No Tudor enclosures here.

Miss Margaret Briggs, who has researched the valley history "and found almost enough to bury me", speaks warmly of the 1974 formation of a new ecclesiastical parish out of the three ancient ones — Woodford, Durnford and Wilsford.

"The river is divisive. It is difficult to get to know people on the other side. This has given the valley a centre."

The parish magazine is called "The Bridge", to show the new link across the Avon. There you may read about Age Concern ("there are still about 12 pensioners who went to school together"), the WI, the Teddy Bears Club and all the parish news.

But it doesn't mention the Japanese Gardens which Major and Lady Anne Rasch keep beautiful at Heale House, the mighty 1832 hickory tree on the vicarage lawn or the last village school in the valley.

It tells you nothing of the chequerboard thatched cottages edging the road, the swans, Robert Edward's water meadows covered in spring flowers — or the deep anxiety that all this could be lost if the Salisbury bypass brings heavy traffic thundering through that valley that calls itself:

A little backwater — and happy to be one.

Above: The village smith at work in the Woodford Valley in the 1950s.

Left: The Wheatsheaf, Lower Woodford's pub.

Woodgreen

THE PEOPLE of Woodgreen have never had to doff their hats to a squire. They are still as proud of that as of their village hall murals, their cricket team and their setting "with the forest as our back yard".

A pretty New Forest village of 450 people, eight miles from Salisbury, it lies between the River Avon and Castle Hill escarpment. There are houses of weatherboard, cob, brick and thatch. Large and small, old and new intermingle. Its thick hedges were planted to keep out animals.

From 1680 until recently, Woodgreen was widely known for Merries — sweet black cherries — and people came to enjoy them on Merry Sundays. Jim Hooper, parish council chairman, well remembers the clattering sound as Jim Angel frightened the birds off the 50-foot merry trees from 4 am. ("Tins tied on to a wire and a rope back to the bedroom window.")

It is hard to believe this was once an unruly village of outcasts as you watch cattle grazing on the green and forest ponies wandering solemnly past the Horse and Groom pub, and the Olde Shoppe (groceries, postcards, dry-cleaning, logs, maps and cassettes).

Woodgreen was first settled in about 1640, but before this law breakers and ruffians sometimes hid there.

Anthony Light tells how in the 1850s Breamore, Downton and Rockbourne "grew weary" of one William Godfrey's misdemeanours. So he was driven out of their parishes and lived in a hollow tree, probably near Woodgreen. Not content with picking, stealing and damaging hedges, he had kept a "young lewde woman as a servant and begat her with childe".

These rough and often unruly forest squatters had names like Witt, Downer, Angel, Harrison, Trim and Chalk. They only became legal in 1801. Until then their shelters "built in a night" were constantly being "put down" by officials. Barns Farm alone has dignified 12th Century origins. It was owned by Breamore Priory.

Until it was "discovered" after the Second World War, Woodgreen was "a village of sturdy self-reliant non-conformists". Many lived off the forest, cutting firewood and turf. They all knew old Granny Cooper, dressed in black, who smoked a long pipe.

A smokey prank was always played on Woodgreen newlyweds. "They used to dig a clod of turf and put it on top of their chimney. It soon smoked them out."

In those days Woodgreen had a butcher and two grocers. Dorothy Light worked in Fairclough's, where "you kept things in drawers behind the counter. Biscuits were weighed out, cheese was cut and sugar was shovelled from the sack". The general store sold paraffin and petrol, Mr Gilbert delivered and Mr Gould ran the Post Office.

At election time long ago, respectable Tory-voting Breamore estate workers dreaded the "wild" Woodgreen Liberal contingent. Sometimes blood flowed at the polling booth.

Next to the thatched cricket pavilion on the Green is the Home Guard ammunition hut ("mostly sandbags and four by twos") and there are dips and hollows where gravel was sold for Breamore roads.

Children still go to Breamore school, but no longer walk; the modern church of St Boniface is run jointly with Hale; there's a Methodist chapel, a beautiful cemetery fringed with forest trees ("the rest camp") and eight new flats for the elderly.

The road towards Hale is depressing, with acres of derelict glasshouses. Once nearly 100 worked for Mr Beckett at Woodgreen Nurseries.

Above: The Avon valley at Woodgreen flooded in winter.

Below: Jim Hooper (right) and Charlie Thorne) at the village bus shelter which has a gate to prevent forest animals using it as a refuge.

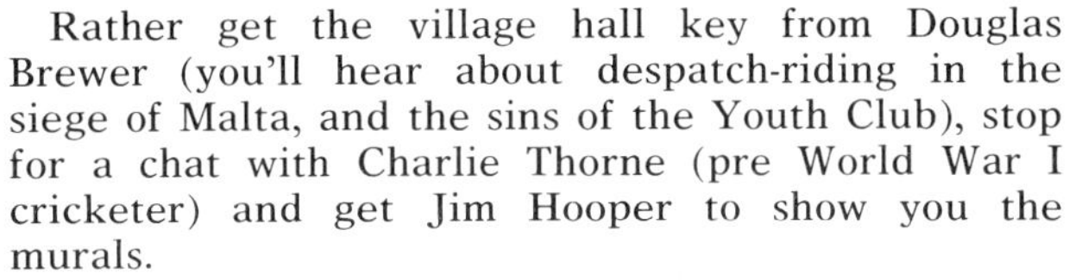

Rather get the village hall key from Douglas Brewer (you'll hear about despatch-riding in the siege of Malta, and the sins of the Youth Club), stop for a chat with Charlie Thorne (pre World War I cricketer) and get Jim Hooper to show you the murals.

Flashback to the 1930s in Woodgreen. Far left: Dan Marks with the Hoopers' cider press. Centre: Mrs Tom Hooper down on the farm. Near left: Mr Poulton, making eel-pots.

Painted in 1931 by Edward Payne and Robert Baker, they captured old Woodgreen — Castle Hill without the pylons, cider-making and merry trees, wooden rakes, bees and goats.

There's folk dancing, milking and poaching, Methodist children in hats, white dresses and short white socks and the flower show. Every face is a portrait.

You'll hear how the young artist sprawled under a tree was married one Saturday in Hale church (to the lady on his right). They cycled to Salisbury for a bread and cheese wedding breakfast, and back to Woodgreen that night. His gift to her of a basket of apples has kept well — on the wall.

Jim Hooper will tell you how Woodgreen showed its disapproval — by Tinpanning. "Bang, bang, bang they went with tins and bars, marching round and round his house for three nights in a row. Then they carried his effigy in a coffin and burnt it on a bonfire near the green."

Though Joby Sivyour plies the woodman's craft, Woodgreen today is better at handbells, WI, cricket and jumble sales — "but you can still have a rare old game of Cowboys and Indians in the Forest".

Left: Bert and Bessie Lawes, of Densome Farm.

A 1950s picnic at Castle Hill, Woodgreen, renowned for its panoramic view up over the Avon valley.